If you've ever doubted God or wondered whether he was with you in the midst of your hardest moments, *Hope in the Dark* is the biblical encouragement your heart desperately needs.

—**Lysa TerKeurst,** *New York Times* bestselling
author; president, Proverbs 31 Ministries

If you're searching for hope, the first step is to look for it in the right places. Craig Groeschel's new book, *Hope in the Dark*, not only shows you where to look but will remind you that you're never really alone—even in the dark.

—**Steven Furtick,** pastor, Elevation Church;
New York Times bestselling author

With mercy, empathy, and deeply rooted faith, Craig Groeschel masterfully touches our hearts by answering Jesus' unending invitation to be honest and ask our toughest questions. Then, courageously addressing the unexplainable pain we experience when tragedy befalls us and life seems so unfair, Craig walks us through the process of falling back into the arms of Jesus, trusting in God's character once again, and drawing closer to God than we've ever been. He helps us turn our doubts into determination, our fears into faith, and our questions into peace. It's a message ministered so well, you will never forget it.

—**Christine Caine,** bestselling author;
founder, A21 and Propel Women

Pastor Craig's words are prophetic, loving, healing, and deeply moving. Being prepared and equipped with truth for those seasons of darkness and hurt and pain is what makes us able to walk through them and stand on the hope we have in Jesus, and Craig lights that path so we are prepared when that time comes. There's no better reminder than the one in this book—that God is good and he always meets us in our hurt.

—**Jefferson Bethke,** author, *New York*
Times bestselling *Jesus > Religion*

Hope in the Dark

Also by Craig Groeschel

Altar Ego: Becoming Who God Says You Are

*Chazown: Define Your Vision, Pursue Your
Passion, Live Your Life on Purpose*

*. The Christian Atheist: Believing in God
but Living as If He Doesn't Exist*

Dare to Drop the Pose (previously
titled *Confessions of a Pastor*)

Daily Power: 365 Days of Fuel for Your Soul

*Divine Direction: Seven Decisions
That Will Change Your Life*

Fight: Winning the Battles That Matter Most

*From This Day Forward: Five Commitments to Fail-
Proof Your Marriage* (with Amy Groeschel)

It: How Churches and Leaders Can Get It and Keep It

*Liking Jesus: Intimacy and Contentment in a Selfie-
Centered World* (previously titled *#Struggles*)

Love, Sex, and Happily Ever After
(previously titled *Going All the Way*)

Soul Detox: Clean Living in a Contaminated World

Weird: Because Normal Isn't Working

What Is God Really Like? (general editor)

Hope in the Dark

Believing God Is Good When Life Is Not

Craig Groeschel

ZONDERVAN®

ZONDERVAN

Hope in the Dark
Copyright © 2018 by Craig Groeschel

Requests for information should be addressed to:
Zondervan, *3900 Sparks Dr. SE, Grand Rapids, Michigan 49546*

ISBN 978-0-310-34295-3 (hardcover)

ISBN 978-0-310-34311-0 (international trade paper edition)

ISBN 978-0-310-34882-5 (audio)

ISBN 978-0-310-34296-0 (ebook)

Craig Groeschel is represented by Thomas J. Winters of Winters & King, Inc., Tulsa, Oklahoma.

Cover design: Micah Kandros
Interior design: Kait Lamphere

First printing April 2018 / Printed in the United States of America

Contents

Part 3: Hope and Glory

A Letter to the Reader

Adrianne Manning is like family to me. She's the most outgoing, gregarious, bubbly, and fun person I know. She has served in my office for many years now, and I love her and her family deeply.

One day years ago, she bounced into my office, beaming with excitement. Part dancing, part shouting, she could barely get the words out. She and her husband, Danny, were expecting. It was an answer to our prayers.

We hugged.

We cried.

And hugged again.

But when she lost her baby, we did the exact same thing. Only the emotions were so much different and deeper.

We hugged.

We cried.

And hugged again.

As a pastor, I see so much loss. It's never easy, especially when it affects someone very close to you. And we did what most everyone does. We asked God, "Why? Why did you allow this to happen?"

And that's when I started writing this book. I wrote. Wrote. And wrote some more. And I didn't tell anyone I was writing. Not my publisher. Not other staff members. Not my friends. I just wrote. With every word, I had Adrianne in mind. And not just Adrianne but everyone I knew who was going through hell on earth and didn't understand why.

If you've read any of my other books, you might notice that this one has a very different tone. I often use humor in my writing because life is so serious. I believe God loves it when we laugh. But you might notice I don't use much, if any, humor in this book. That's because, honestly, my mood was much different when I wrote it. I wanted to wade into some of the deeper issues we grapple with in life and face some of the questions we often don't like to talk about.

After I finished the first draft of the manuscript, I gave it to Adrianne to read. I explained that it was for her. She took the manuscript home and read the whole thing in one sitting. The next day, when she walked into the office, she didn't speak. Instead . . .

We hugged.

We cried.

And then we hugged again.

It was a long time before we talked about the loss of her child. And it was even longer before I told anyone about this manuscript. For years, it sat silently on my computer, stored in an obscure file, mostly forgotten. Then, years later—when I received some bad news about my daughter's health—I decided to pull out that manuscript and look at it again, this time for myself. Oddly, the words I had written for Adrianne helped soothe my own soul.

After praying about it, I decided to show the manuscript to my publisher. Their editors felt the depth of my emotion in the words on the pages, and they believed that this message might be helpful to others.

So I dove back into the manuscript. I updated it some, expanded it. This book is the result.

Just to be clear: this book is not for everyone. If you're living the dream and you're on a spiritual high, stop and praise God for his goodness. I celebrate with you. But, honestly, this book probably isn't for you, at least not in this season of your life. This book is for those who are hurting. For those with doubts. For those afraid that their faith may be failing. For those whose world has grown dark.

On the other hand, if life is closing in on you, if your faith feels stretched to the breaking point, then this book is for you. As you read it, I hope you'll have the courage to enter with me into some of the pain of this world. I hope you will understand why I wrote this with a more serious and reflective tone. I hope you will venture out to the edges with me and wrestle with some of the questions Christians are often afraid to ask. I hope you discover the depths and riches of God's grace that only the valleys of life can reveal.

This book is first for my good friend, Adrianne.

But this book is also for anyone who is hurting and doesn't understand why.

Introduction

When You Want to Trust, but Life Won't Let You

I *want* to believe God cares about me; I really do," she told me, wiping tears from under her darkened, bloodshot eyes. Under the harsh fluorescent lights of the hospital corridor, Marci barely resembled the vibrant girl I remembered, that kid I'd watched grow up in our youth group at church. When she was a teenager, Marci was outgoing, fun-loving, and full of life, even as she was growing more and more serious about her faith, coming early to youth group and staying late. No one loved to worship and talk about God more than Marci.

Then, in her early twenties, Marci met Mark, a great Christian guy with a charismatic personality. They fell in love practically overnight, marrying almost a year to the day after they met. Mark's dynamic personality served him well, helping him land a great sales job. Before long, he was making more money than most other professionals his age. They bought their dream home, and as Mark and Marci served God together at our church, they just knew life couldn't get any better.

But then it did.

After just two months of trying, they learned they were pregnant with their first child. When beautiful little Chloe was born, my wife, Amy, and I joined Mark and Marci at the hospital to thank God for his blessings. Celebrating with them was amazing, all of us thanking God for this wonderful family that he was growing in his presence.

Back then, none of us could see even a hint of cracks around the foundation of their lives. But as the years ticked by, Mark's job had him working longer and longer hours and required ever more frequent travel. Even so, when he came home one day and informed Marci that he was leaving her—for one of her closest friends—she never saw it coming. Devastated, Marci found herself battling on two fronts, coping on the one hand with Mark's betrayal and struggling on the other as a single mom trying to build a new life for herself and Chloe. She took small comfort in thinking that at least things couldn't get any worse.

Until they did.

Chloe, by then in fifth grade, started rapidly losing weight and feeling tired all the time. When the headaches and dizzy spells began, a series of tests revealed the unthinkable—cancer. In just a few short months, Chloe shriveled from being a healthy, popular girl at school into a pale, bedridden patient on a ventilator. Cancer mercilessly ravaged her already weakened body. Chemo didn't even make a dent. Her doctors decided to shift their focus onto doing all they could to make her last days as comfortable as possible.

As I stood there in that bleak hospital hallway, the tireless Marci I had once known was long gone, swallowed up by this weary, defeated woman. She was beyond exhaustion, past depression, dangerously discouraged. She grasped desperately for anything even remotely resembling that bottomless faith that used to come to her so easily. But her unshakeable trust in God was nothing more than a sad memory now. She drew a deep breath, fighting back the sobs. As her forlorn gaze pierced me, it took all the resolve I could muster to remain strong for her.

She sighed. "I *really* want to believe that God is with me right now. I mean, I want to know that he's good, that he cares. I want that so badly, but . . ." Her voice trailed off. This time there was no stopping the tears.

"But, Craig, when I see my baby girl wasting away in there, in so much pain, how can I surrender to a God who allows this? And on top of everything else that we've already been through? I *want* to trust, but I just don't know how."

That one little phrase, "I want to trust," put down roots in my own heart. Everywhere I look, I see people who understand exactly how Marci felt in that cold, sterile hospital. So many people want to believe in God's presence and goodness, but they just have too many unanswered questions. Something in them longs to trust in God—to know him, to feel his presence, to sink into his peace, to believe he's there for them, helping them carry their burdens. They want to pray and know that he hears them. They want comfort. They want to know that he's with them, that he'll protect them. Deep down, they hope God is more than just some kind of made-up cosmic figure that gullible people naively trust. They want him to inhabit more than retreaded clichés thrown around by politicians, activists, and Jesus freaks.

I believe there are a lot of people like Marci, people who once believed God took an active interest in their lives, but they're just not so sure anymore. Maybe he exists, maybe he's sovereign, but does he care? It doesn't feel like it to them. I've even been one of those people myself (more about that later). You may be one right now. Do you ever wonder:

"Where was God when I was being abused? Did he care? If he did, why didn't he do something about it?"

"Why can't we have a baby? There are so many unwanted pregnancies, and so many people seem to have kids they abandon or don't take care of. We go to church. We're good people. We've prayed for years. Why won't God give us a child?"

"What happened to my marriage? More than anything, I wanted at least that to be good. We used to love each other so much, but . . . And Lord knows, I tried as hard as I could. I trusted him. I prayed every day. But now all I have is broken pieces. Why did God let this happen to me?"

"Why was my child born with a disability?"

"Why did I get laid off?"

"Why is everyone I know married and I'm still alone?"

"Why can't I seem to get ahead?"

"Why did the cancer come back?"

"Why have my kids abandoned the faith?"

Do you want assurance that God is there when you need him most, but for whatever reason, you doubt he is?

You're not alone. Throughout the Bible, people questioned God's involvement in their lives. Even Jesus encountered doubters, one of them his own disciple, the original Doubting Thomas. But there's one exchange in particular that Jesus had with a spiritual doubter that I'd like us to focus on. Just like Marci, he was a parent who struggled as he watched his child suffering:

> Jesus asked the boy's father, "How long has he been like this?"
>
> "From childhood," he answered. "It has often thrown him into fire or water to kill him. But if you can do anything, take pity on us and help us."
>
> "'If you can'?" said Jesus. "Everything is possible for one who believes."
>
> Immediately the boy's father exclaimed, "I do believe; help me overcome my unbelief!"
>
> —Mark 9:21–24

Can you imagine the pain this dad experienced? Over and over again, he had to stand by helplessly as his son convulsed, wrestling with an evil spirit that had taken possession of him years before. This loving father would have done anything to ease his son's suffering. But no matter what he tried, his boy still lived in anguish.

As a dad of six children, I don't want to imagine what that must have been like: a powerful evil spirit hurling your child into water like a rag doll or thrashing him into fire. If the father hadn't dutifully protected his son, it's possible that spirit might have already killed him.

It's no wonder this burdened and desperate dad struggled to believe. After trying everything he knew to do, this man said to Jesus the same thing I might have said in his situation: *"If you can do anything, take pity on us and help us"* (v. 22, emphasis mine).

Some Christians might criticize this question. But this dad was at the end of his rope. After doing everything he could think to do, it's possible that he'd finally resigned himself to despair and loss.

He had nowhere else to turn.

Nothing left that he could do.

His hope was gone.

His world was dark.

But then Jesus makes things clear, first by repeating the father's hopelessness in the form of a question—*"'If you can'?"*—and then by challenging him: *"Everything is possible for one who believes"* (v. 23, emphasis mine).

Just think about this. Why didn't Jesus say, "Well, as a matter of fact, I *can* help you"? Or why didn't he say, "I'm the Messiah, the Son of God, and my Father in heaven will heal your son"? Both of those things were true. Instead Jesus put the ball back in the dad's court. While turning to the one and only true God and asking for his help is always a good idea, Jesus said that the key was having trust—faith—that "with God all things are possible" (Matt. 19:26).

The dad's response is even more striking: "I do believe; help me overcome my unbelief!" (Mark 9:24). You hear what he's saying, don't you?

I want to believe.

Lord, I want to believe, but I can't. I'm struggling. *Really* struggling. Help me overcome my unbelief, my doubts.

It's a kind of paradox. This man whose son has been possessed by an evil spirit, a force that's commandeered his son's body and tried to harm him in every way imaginable—for years—says, "I *wish* I could believe, but I don't know how anymore. I'm in such a dark and desperate place, I can't see how things could change for the better. But I want to. I wish I could. Help me believe again, Lord. Restore my hope."

Immediately after Jesus has this exchange with the father, he commands the spirit to leave, and the boy convulses as it comes out, then appears to be dead. "But Jesus took him by the hand and lifted him to his feet, and he stood up" (v. 27). Here's what moves me personally about the story: The boy wasn't the only one healed when Jesus drove out the evil spirit. His father was healed too. Because Jesus drove out the hopelessness that had overtaken him. In the man's sincere request, Jesus could hear the conflicting messages emanating from his battle-scarred heart.

And God still honors this prayer today, if we'll only allow him to.

How about you? Would you like to see your doubt-ridden heart healed? Wouldn't you like to rediscover a deep, abiding assurance in the character, goodness, power, and presence of God? Is that even possible? Could God shine his light of hope into your dark, despairing heart? Could God plant a new seed of faith in your dry soil, that barren wasteland inside you?

Do you want to believe?

SHEDDING THE OLD SKIN OF DOUBT AND DISBELIEF WILL NOT BE easy, especially if your situation's outcome doesn't align with your hopes and expectations. Even though the doctors told Marci's family to prepare for the worst, many of us still believed that God would perform a miracle for her sweet daughter. So we prayed. And we prayed. And we prayed some more. We leveraged social media, seeing what must have been thousands of people—from all over the world—praying that God would heal little Chloe.

Sadly, God didn't do what any of us hoped he would.

Chloe died just three days shy of her eleventh birthday.

And in that moment, what little remained of Marci's fragile faith shattered into a thousand pieces. She shouted. She cried. She sobbed, "Why, God? *Why?* Why would you let this happen to my daughter? Chloe didn't do anything wrong. You should have taken my life, not hers! How can I ever trust a God who would do this to me? How can I believe in a God who would let this happen?"

I didn't pretend to know the whys. I didn't offer pat, pastoral responses. Instead I did what I could do: I prayed *with* Marci and *for* her. I joined together with the multitudes who were already seeking to bring her comfort, to grieve with her, to hold her up.

I have my own hurts, my own losses, my own doubts from time to time, just like you probably do. But I'm still convinced God is with us during our trials, and I want to help restore the faith of people who see their trust in God demolished by that wrecking ball of unbearable circumstances.

It's not easy. I don't have all the answers. But I *can* promise you that I've asked all of those same questions. I've discovered something that I'm praying will become true for you. You can doubt, question, and even struggle in your faith. But instead of finding that the questions distance you from the heart of God, you will discover something else, something much better. Honest questions, sincere doubts, and deep hurts can draw you closer to God than you've ever been before.

THROUGHOUT OUR LIVES, WE ALL REACH POINTS WHERE WE FIND ourselves wrestling with spiritual questions. I knew a man once whose wife of eighteen years was killed by a drunk driver. Sometime after it happened, I was talking with him when he erupted, "If there *is* a God, then there's no way he's good. A good God wouldn't let some drunk idiot kill my wife and let the idiot live! And if God *is* good, then there's no way he's in control of things, or that wouldn't have happened to her! I'm not even sure anymore that God exists. And *if* he does, well, then I don't want to have anything to do with the kind of God that would let something like that happen."

His train of thought was logical. He made some fair points. And the truth is, in the middle of our grief and anger, it's a genuine temptation for us to start seeing God that way. I'd even say that every time we feel pain, our Enemy will try to leverage that to slip a barrier between us and God. But faith isn't about logic. Faith's not a math problem or a language problem or even a philosophy problem; it's a matter of the heart.

I haven't experienced this man's loss. But I ache for him just the same. What's more, I could see that beneath his hurt, he wanted to trust in God. It's just that in that moment, he couldn't reconcile the pain he was feeling with the image of God that he wanted to believe in.

I wrote this book for the many people who are struggling to believe that God cares about them, especially when they find themselves in the middle of a crisis. When you're stumbling through a valley, it's difficult to see the light. You want to believe, but you're having a hard time reconciling the hope-filled message of the Christian faith with what you're seeing around you.

What makes this subject especially personal to me is that my family is living in the middle of an extremely painful trial. Just as the father we read about earlier was hurting for his son, I'm hurting deeply for my second daughter, Mandy. It was only two weeks before Mandy married James that she learned she had infectious mononucleosis, or mono. Even though she eventually overcame this relatively common but uncomfortable disease, her body never fully recovered, and now she struggles with severe physical issues that have baffled the medical experts.

At the age of twenty-one, she had to stop working. We've visited more doctors than I can count. And Mandy continues to suffer.

Even as I'm typing these words, we have just booked flights for Mandy and her husband to travel to the Mayo Clinic, hoping doctors there can diagnose what's causing her physical problems. Here are my current questions for God:

Why her? She loves you, God. She always has.

Why, just before her wedding?

Why won't you heal her?

Why can't we at the very least get a diagnosis?

Not only are we overwhelmed with sincere questions, but we face daily fears. If you knew the details of her physical struggles, you would understand why we are praying many times a day that she's not facing something life-threatening.

So as I'm imagining what challenges you might be enduring, you can know that I'm writing from a place of simultaneous pain and hope. Pain in the moment, and hope for the future. But sometimes the pain seems to yell, while hope only whispers. And sometimes it all leads you to doubt whether God sees your pain and responds and cares.

If you are struggling, you may be able to relate to another spiritual doubter from the Bible, an often-overlooked minor prophet with one of the most difficult names to pronounce: Habakkuk. Habakkuk's name speaks to the same kind of paradox, those same conflicted feelings, that we saw when Jesus spoke with the father of the possessed boy, that my friend Marci felt in losing Chloe. Habakkuk means both to wrestle and to embrace. It's like that kind of hug that wants both to cling to you and to push you away. It's the pain of what you see and feel, and it's the hope that God is still with you. Habakkuk is the kind of heart that wants to believe even as it recoils at the possibility.

If you are struggling, I'm hoping that you are willing to *wrestle*. So many people seem to be seeking a bumper sticker God with whom life is clean, easy, and problem free and answers are clever, even punchy. But life is never clean. It's far from easy. And it's never problem free. That's why I believe putting God into an easy-to-explain box is not only unwise but dangerous. To really know God, you have to wrestle through pain, struggle with honest doubts, and even live with unanswered questions.

So while I won't promise you that God is your copilot or that the Bible says it and that settles it, I will promise you this: if you wrestle with him, seek him, cling to him, God will meet you in your pain.

PART 1

Hide and Seek

1.1

Where Are You, God?

Human beings do not readily admit desperation.
When they do, the kingdom of heaven draws near.
—Phillip Yancey

Painful trials are fertile ground for the seeds of doubt. But life doesn't have to fall apart for someone to start questioning the presence and goodness of God. My first bout with doubt didn't strike during a difficult time; rather it hit during an otherwise ordinary moment in, of all places, a church.

When I was growing up, my family went to church semi-regularly. Naturally, as a kid I just assumed that's what everybody else's families did too. I also assumed that everything I heard about God was true, just as I knew that two plus two equals four and that the Dallas Cowboys were the best team in the NFL. But then, sitting in church one Sunday morning when I was probably about ten or eleven, a buzzing swarm of questions suddenly descended and began to sting my consciousness: "What if all this stuff I've always believed isn't true?

What if God isn't real? And if he *is* real, is he involved in our lives—in *my* life? Does he really care?"

I looked all around, trying to see if anyone else was wrestling with the same intrusive thoughts. No one else, or at least no adults, seemed the least bit antsy or uncomfortable. (Later I learned that appearances can be deceiving.) It wasn't that I suddenly stopped believing what our preacher was saying; honestly, I don't even remember what he was saying. But it was clear that the foundation of my young reality had started to crumble.

The more I thought about the questions I was having, the more questions I seemed to have. If God was in control (as he was supposed to be), then why did so many bad things happen? Granted, my own life was pretty good; I had loving parents and plenty to eat and a warm, dry house. But I was old enough to realize that a lot of people didn't have those things. I had friends whose parents had gone through bitter, angry divorces, and friends who had only one parent at home. I knew kids who got so ill that they had to stop coming to school. The headlines on the news began to penetrate my cartoon-addled mind in a way they never had before, awakening me to bad things happening in the world every day: war, murder, poverty, corruption.

And once those doubts crept in, they lingered. It was as if they had managed to find a secret passage into my mind, and I wondered if I could ever get rid of them. For years I warred with a private spiritual dilemma. If you were to ask me, "Are you a Christian?" I would have said, "Of course." Almost everyone I knew back then would have said the same thing. After all, we weren't Buddhists or Muslims. I claimed to be a Christian, but my life didn't look anything like Christ's. And secretly I wasn't even sure what I really believed about God. If he was real, I assumed, my doubts probably disappointed him—or worse.

It wasn't until college that I truly understood the gospel and what it means to follow Jesus. And for the first time in my life, I started reading the Bible. I was shocked to find that some of the people in the Bible had doubts, just like I did. Thankfully, many of the Bible stories and teachings addressed a bunch of the questions I'd silently wondered about for years. It wasn't as though suddenly I had found a giant flyswatter I could use to bat them all down. It was more like discovering new paths through a familiar forest. I still saw the trees—all of those bad things in the world—but now I also saw a trail leading to the clearing before me. The trees were still all around me, but they no longer stopped me from moving forward.

Until I ran smack into a giant redwood in seminary.

"HERE'S WHAT I THINK OF THIS BOOK!" EXCLAIMED MY NEW Testament professor as he threw the Bible across the classroom in contempt. "It's time you learned the truth about the fairy tales you've been basing your faith on."

You may find that hard to believe, but it's true. While I had some awesome, faith-filled seminary professors, men and women who helped prepare me to be an effective pastor, I had others who were shockingly hostile not only toward all that I'd been raised to believe but even toward God. Just like life itself, my seminary experience was a rollercoaster ride of faith and doubt, despair and hope.

My decision to go there was amazing enough already.

When I felt God calling me into ministry, I was as surprised as anyone. It's not that I was unwilling; it was simply that as a former wild frat-guy-jock-business-major turned Christian, I didn't exactly fit the stereotype I had in my head of what a pastor should look like. By the grace of God, my pastor invited me to join the church staff to help reach some of the younger people the church was missing. My newlywed wife, Amy, and I felt overwhelmed with excitement, honored to be serving God full-time in our church.

When it became obvious that a seminary degree would be an important step in my development—and necessary for my future—I enrolled while still working full-time. Even though the thought of all that extra work and studying intimidated me, I was excited at the prospect of strengthening my faith and becoming better equipped to fulfill all that I felt God leading me to do.

So imagine my shock when I discovered a jaded, cynical attitude among some of my professors and some of the other students. The way they talked, only someone naive or un-educated could really believe in and accept the Bible literally as God's Word.

Without a doubt, my New Testament professor was the worst offender. He didn't believe that Jesus had said or done most of what we find recorded in the Gospels. According to this teacher, Paul wrote only a few of the letters that we attribute to him, and John was most likely coming off a bad drug trip when he wrote Revelation.

I was stunned. Devastated. This guy had more degrees than I had tennis trophies. He was brilliant and even revered in certain theological circles. Someone with his credentials *had* to know what he was talking about, right? Suddenly the questions that I'd thought were dead and gone sprang back to life. Could what he said be true? Was it possible that the Bible wasn't really the timeless, inspired Word of God? Was God real? What if *none* of it was true? All my previous doubts came flooding back into my mind. As a child, I hadn't told anyone because I was afraid of what they might think. As an adult— and a pastor—I was paralyzed with fear. No one could know. What would they think? Nothing could be worse than a pastor unsure of his faith.

So I struggled uphill with my doubts for a while, painfully aware of the many tall trees blocking my path. Eventually, though, I mustered the courage to open up to two people: my pastor and another professor. These wise and mature mentors didn't criticize me or disparage my questions; they gave me permission to wrestle. Then they helped guide me back to truth. What meant the most to me was when they talked openly about their own faith struggles and explained how God had sustained them through their doubts. Their living example taught me that honestly facing my doubts could strengthen my faith and that God would show himself faithful through the process.

My faith may have been on life support, but it didn't just survive; it grew and strengthened. It was as if God made a path through a forest of doubts.

At least until the next obstacle blocked my way.

It's tempting to think that many of us will reach a point in our lives where we'll be forced to question all that we believe, and then after this struggle we'll never doubt again. The truth, however, is that all of us test our beliefs every day. Every time you make a decision about how to respond to someone who is rude to you, your beliefs are front and center. Every time you feel that ache in your body, a reminder of the emergency surgery you're still paying for two years later, you wonder if you'll recover, not just physically but financially as well.

When your car breaks down on the same day that your spouse overdraws your checking account, you face a dilemma about how you'll respond—and more important, about what the basis for your response will be. When you're reading a news app and scan the "word bites" about impending military action against yet another aggressive country, about the latest victim of a serial killer, or about the death toll in a train accident, you're forced to confront your own beliefs—about human nature, about life, and about God.

The more I've lived life and the more I've sought to know and understand God, the more I'm certain that doubts are essential to our maturity as believers. If we want a stronger faith, then we might be wise to allow our doubts to stand as we work through them instead of trying to chop them out of the way.

Judging from what I see in Scripture, I'm convinced that God honors those seekers who sincerely look for the truth, just like that boy's father who wanted to believe so badly that he asked God to help him overcome his unbelief (Mark 9:21–24). Maybe you can relate. You are like so many others who want to believe but feel like life has gotten in the way.

More than a third of the Psalms are prayers or songs of people in pain. These inspired poems often articulate our pain for us when we can't find the words.

> Have mercy on me, LORD, for I am faint;
>> heal me, LORD, for my bones are in agony.
> My soul is in deep anguish.
>> How long, LORD, how long? . . .
> I am worn out from my groaning.
> All night long I flood my bed with weeping
>> and drench my couch with tears.
> My eyes grow weak with sorrow;
>> they fail because of all my foes.
>> —Psalm 6:2–3, 6–7

Can you relate to David's pain? He's exhausted. Worn out. Depressed. And alone. He has cried so many tears, he can't cry any more. It's not that he doesn't believe in God; he absolutely does. He is a man after God's own heart (Acts 13:22). David simply can't understand why the God who has the power to change his circumstances, the one who elevated him from a simple shepherd boy to the king of a nation, won't do it.

The authors of Job, Lamentations, Ecclesiastes, and Jeremiah all express confusion, doubt, and the pain of unbearable suffering endured by faithful believers. Even Jesus questioned his Father's will in the garden of Gethsemane as he wrestled with accepting what he would have to suffer on the cross. And then, on the cross, he cried out in agony, "My God, my God, why have you forsaken me?" (Matt. 27:46).

Maybe in some strange way, God allows us to doubt him sometimes. Maybe he knows that's one of the ways for our faith to grow stronger. One of the best ways.

I understand that's a controversial statement, and you may disagree. But what brought me to that place was my own understanding of the Bible. In addition to the passages of Scripture I've just mentioned, there's one more passage that gives us permission to question God, if we're willing to listen to him in return.

More than 2,600 years ago, Habakkuk asked many of the same questions people all over the world are still asking today. And in his grace, God relieved some of Habakkuk's anguish, even as he left other questions unanswered. But on the other side of his doubts, Habakkuk grew into a person with a richer faith, a faith that may not have developed as fully had he not struggled through his doubts.

Think about it. If you understood everything completely and fully, you wouldn't need faith, would you? But without faith, it's impossible to please God (Heb. 11:6). Why? Because faith and trust must emerge from love, not from a business relationship, a transaction, or some situation in which we have no choice.

Are you willing to ask honest questions? To wrestle?

And more important, are you willing to *listen* for God's answer?

1.2

Why Don't You Care?

I don't know if God exists, but it would be
better for His reputation if He didn't.
Juloo Renard

Most of our crime shows and suspense films are based on
the Old Testament book of Habakkuk. Now, before you
think I'm crazy, hear me out. If you've watched any TV or movies in the past few years, then you've likely encountered some
so-called antiheroes, people who do bad things even though
they have good intentions.

On the big screen, we're no longer surprised when there's
corruption in government or law enforcement. That's now a
standard plot device. We even cheer when the ways that these
antiheroes bend the rules ultimately bring the liars, cheaters,
and murderers "to justice."

Why? Because, like them, we're tired of corrupt, immoral,
unethical people getting away with their crimes. We're sick
of bad guys, whether they're drug dealers bribing their way

out of criminal charges or corporate executives pulling down seven-figure bonuses even as they eliminate thousands of jobs in their companies.

Maybe the reason we like all those superheroes glutting our local Cineplex is because they have the power to defeat villains who have no regard for human life or for playing by the rules. Captain America, Iron Man, and Thor all seem to be doing what we wish God would do sometimes but he doesn't. They don't call them the Avengers for nothing!

Injustice. Corruption. Indifference.

These have been problems almost since the beginning of creation. The prophet Habakkuk is not the first to point it out, but he's definitely one of the earliest and most passionate. Under the reign of King Jehoiakim, Habakkuk witnessed corruption, scandal, and violence that would have made the Godfather blush. Even among God's own people, disputes were often settled by revenge. Officials looked the other way while wealthy criminals dropped coins in their palms. Poor people were often falsely accused of and punished for crimes committed by their rich masters. As a result, some began taking matters into their own hands, not unlike the characters we cheer for on TV and in the movies. It was a mess.

It wasn't that different from our culture. Even if you're not dealing with something painful and unfair in your own life right now, you have to admit, it sure seems like what Habakkuk saw all around him still applies to us today.

How long, LORD, must I call for help,
>	but you do not listen?
Or cry out to you, "Violence!"
>	but you do not save?
Why do you make me look at injustice?
>	Why do you tolerate wrongdoing?
Destruction and violence are before me;
>	there is strife, and conflict abounds.
Therefore the law is paralyzed,
>	and justice never prevails.
The wicked hem in the righteous,
>	so that justice is perverted.

—Habakkuk 1:2–4

I LOVE THE HONESTY IN HABAKKUK'S QUESTIONS: "HOW LONG must I cry for help? God, I *know* you can do something about this. Why don't you?" Habakkuk is reminding God that he's supposed to be a just God and yet he's tolerating the worst sort of violence and injustice.

How do you respond when you experience injustice?

Let's say you're certain you've earned a promotion at work, but your boss overlooks you in favor of someone less devoted. It's unfair. You want to quit, but you need the money. You're stuck.

Or you worked your tail into the ground on your final paper for a class. You're certain it's worthy of an A, so you can't believe your eyes when it comes back a C, dashing your hopes of getting into grad school.

Or you finally get the car you've always wanted, only to be surprised two days later by an eight-inch scratch down the side, courtesy of a lazy, sloppy parker.

MAYBE EXAMPLES LIKE THESE MAKE YOU MAD, BUT THEY'RE JUST things you've learned to accept. They're simply part of life. That's just the way the world works, right? But some other things aren't quite so easy to accept. Things that involve injustice beyond what you ever could have imagined. Deception. Manipulation. Betrayal.

Recently I talked to a friend who had been a faithful pastor for more than two decades. After raising four kids with his wife of almost thirty years, he came home one day to the shock of his life. His wife had decided she didn't want to be married anymore. An old high school flame had contacted her on Facebook. One thing led to another, and she had rekindled her relationship with the man "God had intended for her to marry in the first place."

After she left my friend, the elders at his church started talking. They agreed that in the wake of a scandal like that, he wasn't fit to lead the church. He could resign or be terminated: his "choice."

This poor, battered man sat in my office recounting his losses, and we cried together. He said, "I know God doesn't owe me anything, but now I have nothing. After serving him my entire adult life, how could he allow me to end up divorced and unemployed? It's just . . . just so unfair!"

I couldn't disagree.

Where was the God he had served for all those years? Where is God when someone steals from your business, but then, when they get caught, they declare bankruptcy, so you'll never get back the money they took?

Or what do you say to the wife from your small group at church who loses her husband—a loving, devoted, hardworking guy everyone liked—to a heart attack at age thirty-five? Especially when you think about how many arrogant, mean-spirited people you know who remain healthy and continue to live a long life?

Or what about when someone you loved and trusted for years betrays you? Everyone else thinks she's a strong Christian, which baffles you, because you can't understand how a decent person—much less a follower of Christ—would ever spread gossip about you based on what you confided to her as a prayer request.

Maybe you've tasted the bitterness of injustice firsthand. You did everything you could to raise your kids with love, gentle discipline, and the best you could provide, and yet they've crushed your heart. Even after you've given them your all, now they're addicted to drugs, stealing money from your dresser to get their next fix. All around you, your friends' children seem happy and successful, young professionals graduating from college, getting good jobs, going to church, getting married.

Perhaps you've poured everything you can into your marriage, only to experience a betrayal so unexpected that it feels especially cruel. You thought you knew your spouse, but now . . . this? After all you've been through together, someone at work just had more to offer them? Seriously?

You're devastated, broken, and alone. It doesn't matter what the circumstances are. Sooner or later, we all experience the cruel blows of life. We get kicked in the gut or sucker punched on the chin. Our souls are left to bleed out on the floor.

Sure, you pray. You try to forgive. You read your Bible. You lean on the strong shoulders of your Christian friends and family. You pray some more.

But things only seem to get worse. Life's punches become relentless, one right after another. Your heart becomes battered and bruised, your soul scarred and scabbed with disappointment and sadness. You're numb with rage, paralyzed with grief.

You wonder, "Doesn't God care about what happens to me? Is he just going to let me drown in all these bad things? He's God, so surely he's powerful enough to do something, to change things. Why doesn't he?"

Habakkuk asked these same questions thousands of years ago.

1.3

Why Aren't You Doing Something?

> *Seeing so much poverty everywhere makes me*
> *think that God is not rich. He gives the appearance*
> *of it, but I suspect some financial difficulties.*
> —Victor Hugo, *Les Misérables*

I f only life were like a sitcom.

When I was growing up, there wasn't so much graphic violence and corruption on TV—all those antiheroes we were just talking about. And that's probably just as well, because I imagine my parents wouldn't have let me watch those shows anyway. So I grew up on a steady diet of classic sitcoms: *The Brady Bunch, Happy Days, The Andy Griffith Show,* and the scandalously sexy *Three's Company*.

The formulas were so predictable yet so satisfying. Familiar characters experienced an unexpected problem that provided ample one-liners and silly slapstick situations. Then right before the end, the Fonz or Sheriff Taylor or Alice the housekeeper or Janet and Jack solved the problem, and everything was great again, all in under thirty minutes—and actually, even less than that when you factor in commercial breaks! While I knew this wasn't the way the real world worked, it was hard not to start wishing that life followed a similar script.

At some point, we all notice that the sharp corners of reality have little in common with all those smooth, glossy surfaces of life on television. Maybe it starts at a young age with fairy tales and Disney movies, most of which end pretty well. But when you're being chased not by the Big Bad Wolf but by a whole pack of ravenous wolves with names like Cancer and Bankruptcy and Addiction and Divorce, it's hard to believe in happily ever after.

When you're hit by a drunk driver and you need half a dozen surgeries on your spine just so you can walk again, who would have thought you'd end up addicted to prescription painkillers?

When you slept around some and had that abortion before you became a Christian and then later fell in love with the man who would become your husband, who would ever have imagined that now you wouldn't be able to get pregnant?

When you begged God for a child and he gave you one, who knew that you would lose your spouse to cancer and find yourself working three jobs as a single parent?

When you had a few drinks—far less than everyone else at that party—who would have thought that you'd be the one to end up with a DUI that keeps throwing up roadblocks in your career?

Your life doesn't usually play out in the way you would write your own story. As you're dealing with life's unfairness, even if your mind *is* able to come up with all kinds of resourceful solutions, the tricky part is having the power to do any of those things.

IF YOU WERE GOD, YOU WOULD KNOW HOW THE LATEST EPISODE of your sitcom life should wrap up. You recover from surgery and run your first marathon. You get accepted to your favorite college with a full scholarship. You and your husband pray together through the ordeal of infertility and fall more in love with each other than ever, then adopt a beautiful little girl. You struggle to survive without your spouse, until you meet that amazing, single, gorgeous, godly millionaire in small group at your church.

Of course, if you had the power, you might not *just* provide the happy endings. Maybe you'd go even farther: you'd also punish all those selfish, arrogant, mean-spirited people who seem to get away with murder (literally and figuratively). The drug lords who prey on the most vulnerable, hooking them on a sweet poison that will inevitably kill them. The villains who abuse children and swindle senior citizens. The cheaters in power who rig the system to take advantage of the poor. The monsters who rape women to make themselves feel like men and feed their own desires. The women who manipulate men to get what they want.

If you were God, maybe you'd see to it that these evil people were held accountable. You'd make sure they experienced the same measure of pain, loss, and injury that they've caused. That they suffered at *least* as much as their victims.

But as much as we think we know, the reality is this: we're not God, and we don't know best.

Often when we want God to do something, the solution wouldn't require much of him. A quick nod. A spoken word. An answered prayer. In the grand scheme of things, just a small miracle. If only he would allow me to be rewarded for all my hard work! Or just heal my sick child! Or help my loved one overcome depression! Or break my sexual addiction! Or bring my prodigal child back home! Or at least let me win the lottery!

As we grow to trust God, we have to recognize what I consider to be some of the fundamentals of growing in the Christian faith: Awe. Respect. Reverence. Appreciation for God being God. Acceptance of our limitations as human beings. We can't know everything or see into other people's hearts. We can't know all that has come before in the history of the world. And we sure can't see ahead to how it will all unfold.

But God can.

Like a master storyteller, he is crafting an epic in which he allows each of us to play a significant role. There are no minor characters or bit players in God's story. We're all important. He'll never abandon us, and he's working everything for our good.

So when we're suffering, ranting and raving about all the unfairness of life, we would do well also to remember that there's so much more going on than we can see or understand from our limited perspective. We're seeing only a tiny sliver of a much bigger story, perhaps only one sentence or one paragraph on just a single page.

"GOD, WHY AREN'T YOU DOING SOMETHING?" MIGHT BE THE question that cuts to the heart of our innermost doubts. Basically, we're asking God to reconcile what we believe with what we see in front of us. It's as if the laws of nature that we *thought* were true—you know, things like gravity—suddenly go away. When we suffer at this level, we seem to see apples falling off trees and floating up into the sky.

When our beliefs about God's power, goodness, love, and generosity clash with the awful events that occur in this world, we feel just as untethered as those weightless apples. How does a good God allow terrorists to crash planes into skyscrapers? Or gunmen to massacre students in their schools or viewers in a movie theater? What kind of all-powerful God—I mean, come on—would allow children to be born with AIDS and leukemia and all kinds of other debilitating diseases?

When our eyes witness such heart-wrenching scenes, how can our souls believe that God cares about us?

God understands your pain. And what's more, he invites your questions. He would rather have you yell and scream at him than abandon your relationship with him in icy silence. Feel free to pour out your heart to him, as David did in Psalm 56:8: "Record my misery; list my tears on your scroll—are they not in your record?" God welcomes your anguish and even your anger, but you don't have to stop there. After you've laid bare your hurts and your questions—after you've exhausted yourself pounding against his chest—then listen.

Open your hurting heart to him, and he will speak. Because even though God is almighty and all-powerful and rules over his kingdom, he also cares deeply about you. He loves you, and he will never abandon you. In fact, it's usually at your deepest time of need that he meets you, comforts you, and lifts you into a place where healing can finally begin. But only if you're willing to listen.

1.4

It Seems Unfair

Our vision is so limited we can hardly
imagine a love that does not show itself
in protection from suffering. The love of
God did not protect His own Son.
—Elisabeth Elliot

One of the saddest, most depressing movies I've ever seen would have to be *Sophie's Choice*. I was a kid when it came out, so I didn't see it until much later, after I was grown. By that time, I had heard a lot about it. Meryl Streep won an Academy Award for her role as Sophie, a Polish immigrant living in Brooklyn.

Now, don't get me wrong: it is a superb film, at least as far as the acting and the costumes and the music and the sets go. But the story is beyond sad. Since I can't really recommend it to you, I might as well throw out a spoiler alert and tell you what Sophie's actual choice is all about. Through flashbacks of her agonizing memories, we learn the horrible truth that has haunted this woman.

As prisoners at Auschwitz during World War II, Sophie and her little son and daughter learned to do whatever it took to survive. But then, beyond cruelty, her evil handlers issued the young mother a sickening ultimatum. She must choose between her children: one would go to a work camp and the other to the gas chamber. If she refused to decide, then both children would be killed.

To save one child, Sophie had to lose the other one forever. She made her choice, and years later the pain finally became so unbearable that she took her own life. As I said, it's the best and worst movie I've ever seen. But I've never been able to forget it. As a father of six, I can't even begin to imagine what it would be like to have to choose any one of them over any other.

IF YOU THINK ABOUT IT, LIFE WASN'T FAIR TO JESUS EITHER. HE was perfect in every way. Jesus loved the unlovable. Healed the hurting. Cared for the outcasts. Touched the untouchables. If we look at his story from God's vantage point, Jesus could make the same argument we make: life isn't fair.

It wasn't fair that Jesus had to be whipped, mocked, and beaten. It wasn't fair that Roman guards drove stakes through his wrists and heels, hanging him mercilessly on an instrument of torture and shame. It wasn't fair that they spat on him. Called him names. And laughed when he struggled to breathe. And it wasn't fair that Jesus—the sinless Lamb of God—became the sacrifice for filthy, vile sinners like me.

So when you hurt, when you question, when you burst out

in righteous confusion or anger, you may find comfort that God understands: life is not fair.

Most of us probably don't think much about the pain and anguish that God the Father surely experienced at this loss. Certainly, I don't want to project our human emotions onto God. But since we *are* created in his image, and because we can see how God responds to his people throughout Scripture (expressing love, jealousy, and compassion, to name just a few emotions), I don't think it's a stretch to say that God suffered an enormous burden in sending his only Son to be born into our sin-stained world.

But that was the only way he could build relationship with his earthly sons and daughters. By giving us the gift of free will—which, thanks to Adam and Eve, we wasted no time unwrapping—he also allowed us to live in a world that suffers from our selfishness and sin. He tried the direct approach, but his people just kept wandering away from him, always looking for ways to get what they wanted—idols, power, and deceit, the same things that drove Habakkuk crazy.

So it wasn't fair. A perfect, holy, and just God found himself separated from his imperfect, earthly, sinful creations. By sacrificing Jesus—his own Son—God created a bridge that allows us to know him, to be forgiven of our sins, and to be remade in the image of Christ. But in order to give up his Son (again, not fair), God had to first allow Jesus to suffer in a way that must have felt unbearable to God as a Father, reminding me again of that excruciating decision Sophie had to make.

Philip Yancey, one of my favorite authors on this topic, in his book *Where Is God When It Hurts?* explains God's motivation in making such a sacrifice: "To some, the image of a pale body glimmering on a dark night whispers of defeat. What good is a God who does not control his Son's suffering? But another sound can be heard: the shout of a God crying out to human beings, 'I LOVE YOU.' Love was compressed for all history in that lonely figure on the cross, who said that he could call down angels at any moment on a rescue mission, but chose not to— because of us. At Calvary, God accepted his own unbreakable terms of justice. Any discussion of how pain and suffering fit into God's scheme ultimately leads back to the cross."

When people ask why bad things happen to good people, we need to realize that the worst thing happened only *once*. And Jesus volunteered for it.

WHEN WE'RE BUSY COMPLAINING ABOUT HOW LIFE IS SO UNFAIR, we usually forget that God is also totally unfair. Yes, you read that right.

Not only is life unfair, but in this case God is unfair. To be clear, he's never unfair according to his standards, but he's certainly unfair according to ours. And that's good news for us. Because if he were fair (according to our understanding), then none of us would stand a chance. We are all guilty of sin. We're inherently selfish, both in small, subtle ways and in bold, dramatic ways. When we commit adultery or murder in our hearts, to God we're just as guilty as those who are exposed and convicted of the same acts. At least, that's what Jesus said.

If we got what we deserve, then we would be stuck with ourselves, with no hope of change, no hope of forgiveness, no hope of eternal life in heaven. Just the torment of regret, the terrible loneliness of knowing that we got what we *thought* we wanted—to refuse God's grace and be left alone. We would lose our souls to our own selfish pursuits.

But, thank God, that's not who we are. We are not animals but *people*, created with immortal souls, loved by God so much that he never gives up on us. Even when we get angry and hurt and rage at him. Even when we doubt and question him. Even when we aren't sure what we believe about him. Even when we feel as though we can't trust him. Even when we try to walk away from him.

Certainly, in Habakkuk we see someone—in this case God's own prophet—asking the hard questions. The Hebrew word used to describe Habakkuk's message is *massa*, which means "an ominous utterance, a doom, a burden." Maybe just by his willingness to name the elephant stomping around the room, Habakkuk begins the process of rebuilding a stronger faith. And what does he use? Not just a simple prayer over his dinner but an ominous utterance, a doom, a burden. Sometimes the way back to God isn't a smooth road; it's a road paved with bumps and land mines. But God offers us his Spirit to guide us, lead us, direct us through the maze of doubts and back to the safety of his presence, nature, and goodness.

What if honestly acknowledging your doubts, as Habakkuk did, is your first step toward building a deeper faith? What if embracing your secret questions opens the door for a maturing knowledge of God's character?

What if drawing closer to God, developing genuine intimacy with him, requires you to bear something that feels unbearable? To hear him through an ominous utterance, to trust him in the moment of doom, to embrace his strength when you're weak with a burden? What if it takes real pain to experience deep and abiding hope?

1.5

Crisis of Belief

I know God will not give me anything I can't
handle. I just wish He didn't trust me so much.
—Mother Teresa

Most of us know what it's like to have a mountaintop experience. For many of us, this is how we became Christians
in the first place. We had an amazing experience in which we
felt God's presence in a real, tangible, all-consuming way. We
sensed his love, his grace, his power, his Spirit. In that moment,
we knew that we wanted to spend the rest of our lives on this
earth, as well as the rest of eternity, serving him, pursuing him,
and making him known.

That's certainly my story. After reading about God's grace
in the second chapter of Ephesians, I walked alone to a place
of solitude just outside the softball dugout at my university.
Though I could never adequately describe it, God's presence
was as real to me there as the lunch I had just eaten in the cafeteria. I could *feel* his love. *Sense* his forgiveness. *Hear* his still,

small voice calling me to himself. And that's when it happened. I knelt down, and in my own words, I asked him to take my whole life. When I stood up, I was a different person.

And the spiritual transformation began!

It didn't matter where I was; I believed that God was with me. I shared my faith with my fraternity brothers, with my professors, with my teammates, and even with my opponents. It seemed like God answered every prayer. Every Bible verse I read seemed to be written just for me. And everywhere I went, it seemed like God gave me the words to say and showed me a difference that I could make.

Initially, being a Christian can feel like this amazing experience. You have these powerful times of praying and studying the Bible. Each day, the words of the Bible seem to jump off the page, ministering to you in just the perfect way. Sermons seem to be especially for you, directly addressing something important that you're going through, or thoroughly explaining a Scripture you just read. Then you see the same verse on someone's social media feed, and you know that God is speaking to you. When you get in your car, your favorite song comes on the radio, and it feels like God played it just for you. You feel an urgency to help your non-Christian friends, and God constantly gives you the right words to say. You know he's with you. When you're in a rush at the mall, a parking spot opens up right in the front row.

That's when you know you're on top of the mountain.

Then, at some point, life starts to creep back in. And God's presence seems to fade. Without even realizing it, you have come down from the mountain, back to the real world, and your faith doesn't seem quite so amazing anymore. You still believe in God, still go to church, still try to read the Bible and pray when you have time. But the sermons aren't always just for you. Your favorite song isn't on the radio anymore. And the best parking spots are all taken.

Suddenly life isn't going as you planned or hoped. Your prayers feel flat and stale. It seems like God has stopped listening. Someone betrays you. God doesn't feel as close as he once did. You feel disoriented, uncertain where you stand with God, or whether you're still standing at all. You were up on the mountaintop, and now you're down in the valley.

If you've never been there, I hope you never are. But I suspect you might know something about what I'm saying. You woke up one day only to realize you were burned out. Discouraged. That little orange light comes on, telling you that your faith tank is dangerously low. It's at this time that we hit what author and marketing guru Seth Godin calls "the dip," which he describes as that learning curve valley that you have to slog through to mature in your career from novice to master. While Godin uses this image to make shrewd observations about marketing and advancing within your chosen field, I hope to apply it in a different way: to depict that dark valley you have to walk through when you come down off the mountaintop.

In his book *Experiencing God*, author Henry Blackaby describes this valley as a "crisis of belief," a season of struggling and doubting God and his goodness in our lives. Usually, this crisis is ignited by a specific trigger, such as a serious physical challenge, a financial setback, or a relational disappointment.

Often the trigger is something unexpected or even unthinkable. Sometimes several smaller but challenging events overlap, and the combined burden becomes a crushing weight that causes a person's faith to collapse. Didn't Christ say that his burden was light and his yoke was easy (Matt. 11:30)? Suddenly, getting out of bed in the morning feels intimidating. You can't imagine how you're going to get through the rest of this morning, let alone an entire day. Where's God now?

In those moments, faith seems irrelevant. When the *Titanic* is sinking, it's hard to enjoy a game of shuffleboard on deck or to appreciate the string quartet playing music on the bandstand. When you don't know whether the radiation and chemo will work or where the money's going to come from or when you'll see your child again, it's hard to believe that praying, trusting, and hoping will make a difference. It's hard to keep the faith when you have so little control over everything else in your life.

Sometimes the pain is so intense that all you can think about is relief. Everything in you just wants it to stop. Because the immediate hurt is so extreme, instead of thinking about Jesus, you may just be thinking about getting out of the pain you're in. But this can become a pivotal moment in your faith journey. This is when you can experience the depth of God's grace in a way that's impossible during better moments. His presence is real in your pain. And it might become more real in this valley than it was on the mountaintop, if you can recognize that the way is *through*, not out.

Perhaps that's why Blackaby sees this crisis as so vital, a requisite part of the Christian faith. If we're going to become stronger in our faith, more committed to God, more in love with Jesus, then our beliefs will be tested. They *must* be tested. Blackaby explains, "Will God ever ask you to do something you are not able to do? The answer is yes, all the time!" People may tell you that God won't give you more than you can bear. While they probably mean well, that's simply not true. The Bible does say that God won't let you be *tempted* beyond what you can handle (1 Cor. 10:13). But he often gives you more than you can handle, so you can learn to depend wholly on him.

Those words can be difficult to read and digest when you're hurting. Believe me, I understand. Remember: I've been there. And as a pastor, I often walk with people through the lowest points in their lives. It's never easy. But God's faithfulness is always evident.

I spent a considerable amount of time with a guy I'll call Martin. As a brand-new follower of Christ, Martin felt guilty for having previously embezzled a lot of money from his employer. After discussing the situation with trusted advisors, Martin decided that the right thing to do was to confess his crime and hope for the best. Unfortunately, the outcome fell closer to the worst.

Martin's company pressed charges. Even though he admitted to the crime and agreed to repay the money, Martin was sentenced to seven years in prison. Seven years. For confessing and doing what was right.

Some people might have gotten mad at God. But Martin

told me he'd never been closer to God than when he was in prison. During that time, his spiritual roots grew deep. And his spiritual fruit multiplied. Every time I received a letter from Martin during his prison stay, it was always signed, "His grace is enough, Martin."

WHEN MY DAUGHTER MANDY WAS CHOSEN TO TELL HER STORY to teenagers, I was bursting with pride to hear about her faith in Jesus. She did such a good job that Christine Caine, a well-known international speaker, invited Mandy to speak at a huge conference for women. All of us could sense that God was opening doors for our special twenty-one-year-old follower of Jesus. Then Mandy got sick. I mentioned earlier the mono. But that was only the beginning. What followed were far too many complications to list here. One minute, we were together on the mountaintop. And the next, we were tumbling end over end in an avalanche into the valley.

While Mandy's faith doesn't seem to have wavered, as a dad, I've had some difficult conversations with God. So when I encounter people who have deep faith struggles, it's easy for me to patiently hear them out. I have compassion for them that I didn't before. And even when I talk to people who have different views on the existence or goodness of God, my approach to sharing with them has changed over time. Through years of maturing, I've learned that it's not our job to force our beliefs down others' throats until they echo back what we want to hear. No, our job is to challenge their categories by doing the same things Jesus did: loving them, challenging them, accepting them, and forgiving them.

I think Christianity has gotten a bad rap in the last few decades because so many Christians try to pretend they have everything figured out. This includes the problem of pain in the world. Let me say again that I'm not against developing a theological understanding of evil in the world, of human suffering, and of the goodness of God. That's very important. It's just that when you're standing in front of a father whose son has just been killed in war, or a woman who just learned that her cancer has returned, theology—or at least the ability or need to explain it—isn't necessarily our first objective. When words don't work, remember that presence does. Love does. An embrace does.

That's the beauty and power of the incarnation. God didn't shout his love from heaven. He showed us his love on earth as he became one of us in the person of his Son Jesus. When someone is in the valley, rather than trying to explain what's happening, sometimes we are better off listening. Rather than preaching, we focus on loving. And in those moments of quiet presence, God often reveals himself in ways that go beyond our human ability to understand.

Unless our own suffering draws us closer to God, it's hard to offer genuine compassion—and hope—to others. When we aren't connected to others' pain, it's tempting instead to offer them bumper sticker platitudes and pat answers designed to keep our own fragile faith intact. Some people even go so far as to tell those who are suffering that it's because of sin in their lives or because they don't have enough faith or because they're simply getting what they deserve. What a terrible, dangerously hurtful, *unbiblical* response! Nowhere do I see Jesus condemning people who are hurting; I see him only allowing his grace to convict their hearts and convince them of their need.

Our world is broken. Because we live in a world where our free will has opened the door to our spiritual enemy, we will all continue to experience painfully hard, terrible, unexpected events in our lives. It's not that growing mature in our faith exempts us from these events. (The opposite might be closer to the truth.) It's simply that we've experienced enough pain and grown so much closer to God—even in spite of our pain—that our faith has been strengthened, deepened, and matured for the next tough time.

Author and scholar C. S. Lewis explains it this way: "I'm not sure God wants us to be happy. I think he wants us to love, and be loved. But we are like children, thinking our toys will make us happy and the whole world is our nursery. Something must drive us out of that nursery and into the lives of others, and that something is suffering."

HABAKKUK KNEW FIRSTHAND WHAT WE'RE TALKING ABOUT. HE clearly slipped into the valley and experienced a crisis of belief. What he saw and what he knew about God didn't line up. It was just hard for him to grasp that the God of Israel would sit on his hands and allow the kinds of atrocities that Habakkuk was witnessing. He wrote,

LORD, are you not from everlasting?
My God, my Holy One, you will never die.
You, LORD, have appointed them to execute judgment;
you, my Rock, have ordained them to punish.
Your eyes are too pure to look on evil;
you cannot tolerate wrongdoing.
Why then do you tolerate the treacherous?
Why are you silent while the wicked
swallow up those more righteous than
themselves?

—Habakkuk 1:12–13

Can you feel his pain? His doubts? His sense of injustice? Basically, he asks, "Aren't you the eternal, all-powerful God? Why don't you *do* something?" He goes on to remind God that God was the one who chose the people who are now punishing the innocent. In an almost sarcastic tone, Habakkuk says, "You can't even *look* at evil, but you allow it." Like many of us, Habakkuk can't figure out why God doesn't do what he thinks God should do.

Keep in mind: Habakkuk is a man who loves God! This is in the Bible, not in an angry blog post from some smug person who hates Christians. Habakkuk didn't hold back.

And neither should we.

God can handle any question we dare to ask him. He may not answer in an audible, booming voice. (Most likely, he won't.) But he isn't angry with us when we do ask. It's not as if he's going to storm out of the room when we throw a tantrum.

He understands. Even as we're pouring out our emotions, he wants to draw us closer to himself.

We have his permission to speak freely.

Sometimes I think we're afraid of expressing our questions not because we're worried about God's response but because we're worried about our own. We're afraid to say what we're feeling, deep down in the dark corners of our souls. We're terrified that if we admit how we're truly feeling, then our faith will crack. But the opposite is true. It's when we suppress the pain of what we're experiencing, stuffing it down and denying it, that our faith becomes so hard and brittle that it breaks.

Maybe this explains why, when some of us slip into the valley, we try to force our way back up to the mountaintop. We want that closeness we used to have with God. But denying that things are the way they are, refusing to believe the truth, is like trying to run up a sand dune.

A woman who's been downsized might say, "It's okay that I lost my job. I know that God can provide a better job. So I'll just sit here and wait for it to come to me."

Or a man might refuse to believe his doctor's diagnosis. "Nope. Not me. I'm just going to pray and trust that God will heal me. I don't need to seek any kind of treatment."

Don't misunderstand: I'm not discounting that God can (and does) provide jobs out of the blue and heal people miraculously. But when we retreat and refuse to feel the pain of our disappointment, then we're not *really* trusting him. We're using him. And maybe missing greater opportunities for growth. Peaks are nice, but you don't see many farms on mountaintops.

Why? Because things grow better in valleys. Your time in the valley may not be pleasant, but it's in the valleys of life that you grow closer to God and stronger in your faith.

I agree with C. S. Lewis that God's highest agenda is not our immediate happiness. I believe that God is much more committed to our eternal joy, our spiritual growth, and the condition of our hearts. This means that we need to grow out of spiritual infancy into a richer, ever-maturing belief in a God who is infinitely wiser than we are. We need to learn to trust him even when we can't feel him, believe in him even when he doesn't make sense, and follow him even though we're not sure where he's leading us.

"Consider it pure joy, my brothers and sisters, whenever you face trials of many kinds, because you know that the testing of your faith produces perseverance. Let perseverance finish its work so that you may be mature and complete, not lacking anything" (James 1:2–4). As counterintuitive as this may sound, I don't think James is telling us just to suck it up and keep going. I think he is reminding us of that bigger picture, that larger story, that sense that something greater is going on than the trial we find ourselves caught up in. Here's something curious: James doesn't tell us that we can't ask God what's going on; he tells us only to count our problems as joy.

The point, as Habakkuk seems to have grasped, is asking honest questions while also trusting God and his Word. Think about it: you can have a sincere faith in God even as you are wrestling with unanswered questions. God is big enough to handle it. And he loves you enough to be patient with you as you learn about parts of his character that were too deep for you to comprehend before your crisis of belief.

Apparently, this prophet was also willing to listen when God responded—which, as we're about to see, God did. The good news is that God will meet you in your moment of greatest need. Just as he responds to Habakkuk, he will respond to you. In fact, God has plenty to say to us about how we should face our trials. Again, he never says we can't ask him our honest questions. On the contrary, Jesus said, "Ask and it will be given to you; seek and you will find; knock and the door will be opened to you. For everyone who asks receives; the one who seeks finds; and to the one who knocks, the door will be opened" (Matt. 7:7–8).

So if you have questions, ask away.

Just be prepared when God answers.

PART 2

Lost and Found

2.1

Listen

Listen to your life. All moments are key moments.
—Frederick Buechner

Recently I was sitting in my favorite chair at home, going through my sermon notes, checking email, and responding to a friend's texts, when my wife, Amy, came in and asked if she could talk to me about the kids' schedules for the rest of that week.

"Sure," I said. "Go ahead. I'm listening."

"I can come back when you're finished," she said. "I didn't know you were working on something."

"No, it's okay," I repeated. "Just finishing up a few things." I still had not looked up at her for more than two seconds.

So Amy sat across from me and began downloading a week's worth of soccer games, piano lessons, dance recitals, and youth group events. And when you have six kids, that's a lot!

"Uh-huh," I said, still not looking up. "How can I help?"

"Craig," she said, "you haven't heard a word I've said." She didn't sound angry, just a little annoyed, which is perfectly understandable when the person you're talking to is mentally engaged elsewhere.

"I heard you," I said. "Joy needs to be at the church on Wednesday after school, and you need me to take Stephen—"

She interrupted, "Oh, I know that you *heard* me. But you weren't *listening.*"

Ouch.

She was right. I heard, but I didn't listen. My ears responded to the sound waves that were her words, but their meaning and significance didn't make it to my already over-engaged brain. Sure, we all tend to hear but not listen—multitasking seems to have become our cultural default—but that doesn't let me off the hook. Few people just sit and watch TV anymore. Most watch TV *and* look at Instagram *and* text friends *and* respond to email *and* update calendars *and* pretend they're listening when someone tries to engage them. Be honest with yourself: when was the last time you sat and *just* had a real, live conversation with someone else, in which you took turns and genuinely listened to what they said? No devices. No TV. No music. No distractions.

No wonder it's so hard for us to listen to God.

AS WE SAW IN PART 1, HABAKKUK BOLDLY ASKED GOD ALL THE really hard questions that were on his heart. He may have known that sometimes just allowing yourself to ask these questions can take you a long way toward reconnecting with

God and learning to trust him. It's hard to love someone—even the Creator of the universe—if you're holding grudges and hiding your true feelings. Habakkuk clearly loved God, but that didn't keep him from respectfully challenging God (not testing him; there's a difference) with a request to help him understand the huge gap between what he believed and what he saw all around him.

Once the prophet had finished asking his questions, he knew it was time to listen. The same is true for you. Habakkuk wrote, "I will *stand at my watch* and station myself on the ramparts; I will look to see *what he will say to me*, and what answer I am to give to this complaint" (Hab. 2:1, emphasis mine). I love these images. I will stand at my watch and look to see what God will say to me. As basic and obvious as this may seem, sometimes the reason we're not getting answers to our questions is that we're not willing to pause and wait long enough for God to reveal himself to us.

Sometimes when we rave and rant, what we really want is simply to vent our emotions, not to engage in a conversation. When we allow our anger, doubt, and fear to control us, our questions can drown out what God wants to say back to us.

Other times, we may pose our questions to God, but then, because we're so preoccupied with the many things that are pulling at us, we don't pause to listen for his response. As in my one-sided conversation with Amy, we hear but we don't listen.

Why don't we slow down to hear God's still, small, comforting voice? Honestly, I think it's because too many of us are overwhelmed. We're so busy juggling work, home, school, church—not to mention whatever crisis ignited our doubts in the first place—that we don't take time to stop, to quiet our hearts before God in silence.

The writer of Psalm 46:10 quotes God: "Be still, and know that I am God."

When was the last time you stopped everything and just sat completely still, listening for God's voice?

Notice what God did *not* say: "Be *busy*, and know that I am God."

He said, "Be still."

Be.

Still.

And listen.

How do you actually listen to God? You can open his Word and let his Spirit bring truth to life. God speaks through circumstances, if you pause long enough to reflect. He speaks through people, offering divine wisdom from heaven. And he can speak directly to you through his Spirit. When you belong to him, spend time with him, and quiet yourself before him, you will learn to recognize his voice.

Think about it this way: one of the unexpected benefits of going through a difficult season is that it gives us the chance to stop and reevaluate our priorities. In fact, some say that the Chinese word for crisis uses two characters: one means "danger," and the other means "opportunity." When Mandy started battling her illness, the challenges it presented prompted us to spend more time with her and her husband. And the time we spent with them inspired us to be more intentional with our other five children. Suddenly we found ourselves purposefully slowing down from the constant pressures of life and embracing the people we value most. When hard things happen, we often see more clearly what means the most to us. Spending time alone with God should be at the top of our list, even if the conversation with him will be a difficult one.

However, as Habakkuk discovered, when you ask God the tough questions, you have to be prepared to listen to his answers, even if you don't like them. Hopefully, if you are hurting and you press into God's presence, he will direct you, guide you, and comfort you. But in Habakkuk's case, God had other things to do first. And the news would be difficult to hear.

God said, "Look at the nations and watch—and be utterly amazed. For I am going to do something in your days that you would not believe, even if you were told. I am raising up the Babylonians, that ruthless and impetuous people, who sweep across the whole earth to seize dwellings not their own" (Hab. 1:5–6).

That's stunning. Shocking. And hard to swallow. God's raising up the enemy?

Basically, he told Habakkuk, a guy he had chosen to be his prophet and therefore his messenger to the Jewish people, "Here's the thing: you're right—my people have really sunk to a new low. And while it may feel like I'm letting things slide, really I'm not. In fact, I'm going to have to destroy the people of Israel because they're so wicked. And I'm going to use the Babylonians to do it."

I imagine Habakkuk's jaw dropping as he expressed

some deep, theologically mature response, like, "Say what?" Essentially, God said that things would get worse before they'd get better. The Babylonians were notorious for being ruthless, violent, and aggressive in their relentless conquest of other tribes and nations. Corruption and violence among the Israelites might have been bad, but it was nothing compared with that of the Babylonians. It would almost be like us asking God why he allows so much injustice in our country, only to have him tell us that he was going to allow foreign terrorists to annihilate us.

When times are tough, the last thing we want to hear is that they're about to get tougher. But we know that real life doesn't always go the way we want it to. So what now?

When you're going through a season of struggling with God, remember: Habakkuk's name means both to wrestle and to embrace. You can wrestle with God about all that you don't like, yet simultaneously embrace him because he is good and trustworthy. It really comes down to how we respond to a crisis of belief. Usually when a person enters that valley, they go to one of two extremes.

Many want to return to their last spiritual high, that mountaintop experience in which everything with God seemed great. He was answering their prayers, life was good, and their faith felt strong. They deny all the doubts undermining their faith, telling themselves, "I'm going to pretend this crisis isn't happening right now. I know if I can just get back up on that mountaintop again, everything will be all right."

I work out at the gym with a guy who recently lost his job. He was convinced that God would bring him another one, so he never submitted any applications or put out any feelers. Eventually he had to move in with his buddy and sleep on his couch. When I told him about a lawn company that was hiring, he explained that he didn't like manual labor and that he was certain God would give him a better job. I sure can't fault him for his strong belief in God's providence, but sometimes we have to come down off the mountain and let God help us deal with the real world.

Some people slide into the valley and decide to descend even farther. They say, "Okay, God, if you're not going to do what I know you *could* do, then forget you! I'm going back to the life I used to know. If you *could* help, but you're not helping, then you must not be good, so I can't trust you." They wrongly assume that God must not love them if he's not willing to do what they want him to do to alleviate their suffering.

My friend Ronny falls squarely in the middle of this second category. When Ronny was in grade school, he found his mom dead in her bathtub. (Tragically, she had drowned during a seizure.) We can only imagine the unfathomable pain of a little boy finding his mom's lifeless body. How many nights, weeks, and months did he cry himself to sleep, possibly even blaming himself for not checking on her? Willing to give anything to have her back.

Today Ronny is older than his mom was when she passed away, but to this day he refuses to talk to God. I'll never forget the pain I saw in Ronny's eyes when he told me, "I *want* to believe that God loves me, but how can I believe in a God who would let that happen to my mom? If there *is* a God, and he allows things like that, then I don't want to have anything to do with him."

Thankfully, there is a third option. If, like Habakkuk, we're willing to lean into the hardship we're experiencing and wrestle with how God might use it to achieve his purposes, then we can begin to climb out of the valley. You have to remember, though, that just because things aren't going your way doesn't mean God isn't still working. But I will admit that from a human perspective, his interventions may seem mysterious or even capricious. Let me give you two examples from my own life. The first story is about an answer to prayer—one that is miraculous but not that important in the grand scheme of things. The second is about a far more important personal prayer request and need. It's something God could easily do, but as of this writing, he hasn't.

First, after twenty-three years of marriage, Amy lost her wedding ring. Since I was mostly broke when I proposed to her, the ring wasn't very expensive, but it would be impossible to place a dollar amount on its sentimental value. Amy was beyond brokenhearted. She prayed and prayed and prayed that God would help her find it.

It didn't turn up.

Eight months later it was a Sunday afternoon, and we were talking together about the message I'd just taught at church. It was all about God's ability to restore. Over and over during that message, I had said, "God can help you find what you didn't mean to lose." So Amy decided to pray again, using that key statement from the sermon. She told me that she'd give anything for God to just show us where it was.

And that's when the craziest thing happened. I felt this uncontrollable urge to get up. I walked past the sofa and past two chairs and to the far side of the room, where there was a single chair by itself. I lifted the light-blue cushion, and right there underneath it was a shiny piece of jewelry. It was her missing ring!

I had never seen Amy dance like that before.

You may scoff and say it was a coincidence, but I believe God showed me exactly where we could find Amy's lost ring.

God answered our prayers.

Now, here's where things get confusing for me. For more than ten years now, Amy has suffered from chronic urinary tract infections. These frequent attacks are so painful that they shut down all her normal activity. She's tried every supplement, diet, vitamin, health drink, and suggestion you could imagine. She's been to the best doctors and has had two surgeries. We've prayed for healing more times than we can count. And yet God still hasn't healed her. Why is it that God would help us find an inexpensive, completely replaceable piece of jewelry, but he won't take away her chronic pain? Why would he answer some prayer that's so much less important, while at the same time allowing our greater cry for help to go unanswered?

Maybe you can relate.

Although we don't understand, we continue to believe God, listening for his voice and waiting on his answer. And just like

Habakkuk, we will cling to God and trust him, even when he doesn't seem to make sense.

The I-want-to-believer who will continue to embrace God, even though things may not get any better at first, will grow much closer to God than he or she was in the past. If you look at the people you know who are closest to God, often they're the very ones who have been through the most difficult times, and God has proved himself faithful to them. Their intimacy was forged through conversations with him—asking him and then listening patiently.

I've never seen this more powerfully than with one of my best friends, John. About two years ago, John noticed a ringing in his ear that grew louder and louder until it was unbearable. After several visits to various doctors, John was diagnosed with an incurable condition called tinnitus. On a scale of 1 to 10, with 10 being the worst, his condition is a 9.5. Many people with cases less severe than John's can't stand the pain and noise, and they end up taking their own lives. My buddy will tell you honestly that he didn't want to live but was determined to overcome this nonstop nightmare.

One day, John flew to Atlanta to meet with one of the nation's best tinnitus doctors. One reason this doctor is so good is because he suffers from the same condition. He gave John a custom-fitted earpiece designed to create a competing noise that helps drown out the constant freight train sound in his head. But, the doctor admitted, it probably wouldn't do much to help in John's extreme case. This wise doctor explained that the best thing John could do was to serve others. Yes, you read that right. The way to forget about the pain is to help other people, so you forget about yourself.

And that's exactly what John did. On top of his usual prayer and Bible study time, John started doing more—way more. He and his wife started a small group and began pouring into others spiritually. They started serving in different roles in the church, and they "adopted" a single mom and her kids to help them climb out of a very bad situation. John tells me all the time that the buzzing sound in his head is just as bad as it's ever been, but it doesn't bother him as much as it used to. Occasionally through tears, John tells me that he's never been closer to God than he is now. And though he would never choose this road nor wish it on his worst enemy, John is thankful for it, because his nightmare condition has helped him come to know God more intimately.

John's story reminds me of one in the New Testament, in which the apostle Paul experienced what he referred to as "a thorn in my flesh" in his second letter to the church at Corinth. Paul said he had asked God over and over to remove it. But God didn't. Paul describes this agonizing prayer: "God, I know you can do something about this. Please do. Take it away. Remove it. I'm pleading with you, please take it away from me" (2 Cor. 12:7–8, my paraphrase).

Maybe you can relate. "Please heal my loved one." "Please help me get a better job." "Please help me get accepted into my favorite school." "Please save my dad." "Please take the depression away." "Please stop my migraines."

But the thorn remained, and Paul came to understand that

God was allowing it in order to help Paul stay humble and dependent on God, and to do something even more amazing than simply taking it away. God told him, "My grace is sufficient for you, for my power is made perfect in weakness" (2 Cor. 12:9). It's almost as if God were telling Paul, "Look, I could take away this thorn for you. But if I did, then you'd miss out on drawing closer to me and finding a deeper appreciation of my grace."

Paul got it. He wrote, "Therefore I will boast all the more gladly about my weaknesses, so that Christ's power may rest on me. That is why, for Christ's sake, I delight in weaknesses, in insults, in hardships, in persecutions, in difficulties. For when I am weak, then I am strong" (2 Cor. 12:9–10). Paul didn't just hear God's response; he listened. And that subtle difference changed the very fabric of who Paul was, just as it changed my friend John.

It can change you too. In your most desperate moments, God's presence can sustain you. Just as resistance in the gym makes your muscles grow stronger, resistance in life strengthens your faith in God. Over time, as you grow in the grace of God, what normally would have rocked your world becomes something you can take in stride, knowing God is with you and will carry you when you are weak.

You may not want to hear that right now. If you don't, that's fair. I'm guessing this message wasn't what Paul wanted to hear. But it served a purpose higher than Paul might have been able to understand at the time. Without Paul and his influence, the Christian faith as we know it might not exist today.

That means this ordinary man who refused to believe that God had abandoned him could be at least partially responsible for the faith in Christ that we still see around us today.

But seeing God's impact through you is hard to do when you're in pain.

All our lofty principles and spiritual convictions seem to blur when we're looking through the cracked lens of a broken heart.

That's when you take the next step by faith.

Maybe you've been asking God for what you need. That's perfectly reasonable; God wants us to reach out to him. But are you willing to listen to what he has to say to you, even if his answer isn't what you want to hear? Keep listening. God will not abandon you in your time of need; he will tenaciously hold you close and carry you through your pain.

2.2

Write

If we desire our faith to be strengthened, we should not shrink from opportunities where our faith may be tried, and therefore, through trial, be strengthened.
—George Mueller

How do you react when life crashes in on you? What are your default responses, the things you run to for comfort, relief, or escape? If that sounds like I'm asking about your addictions, then I probably am, because these are usually built around the idols we turn to when things get hard. For some people, it may be comfort food. For others, it may be trying to escape through drugs, partying, TV, or even just killing time piddling on your phone, your tablet, or your computer. Whatever it is, your means of escape often only makes things worse.

A close friend of mine found himself having marriage problems. Rather than running to other Christians or running to God, he turned to alcohol. And what first numbed the pain slowly began to kill his judgment. After his second DUI, he finally admitted that he might need help.

For most of us, trying to avoid a situation—or looking else-where for comfort—only makes matters worse. We end up even more frustrated, because nothing changes. We may even feel guilty for not being strong enough to deal with whatever thorn has gotten under our skin. Ultimately, we run even farther away from the only one who can truly help us. Whether you're in denial, quoting Bible verses, trying to backtrack to your last spiritual high point, or abandoning your faith altogether, you're still avoiding the elephant in the room.

Until we're willing to have that honest conversation with God, that wrestling match that Jacob experienced, which both wounded him and forever changed his identity, we will never know peace. But how?

Habakkuk helps guide us through the valley with three specific actions. First, as we just saw, Habakkuk questioned the apparent injustice of God. Then he decided to stop and listen to God as he learned of God's intent to destroy his people using the evil Babylonians. Next, he took notes. God told Habakkuk, "Write down the revelation and make it plain on tablets so that a herald may run with it" (Hab. 2:2). Finally, and this may be the hardest action of all, Habakkuk realized that he needed to wait on the Lord's timing. He had to trust that God knew the best time to lead his people back to the mountaintop.

NOT THAT I'M REALLY OLD—AT LEAST, NOT YET—BUT IT SEEMS like every time I go to the store, I forget something unless it's written down. Yeah, I'm *that* guy jogging from the checkout lane back to aisle 12 for a bottle of ketchup. Even if it's only two or three items, unless it's on paper or the notepad app on my phone, I seem to lose track of whatever Amy asked me to buy. Was it chocolate ice cream with cherries and nuts or chocolate chip ice cream with nuts and cherries? You'd think it wouldn't make a difference, but it does.

So I've learned to write it down.

When Habakkuk wrote down his conversation with God, including God's promise to deliver his people by first allowing them to be trounced by the Babylonians, he was creating a public record.

Why would God want him to do that? Part of the reason should be obvious. By having his words written down, God ensured that future generations—including our own—would see his promises fulfilled. Basically, God told Habakkuk, "Write it down so that when I prove myself just and true, everyone can remember that I am a God of my word."

When God says something to you, record it, because your spiritual enemy is an expert at stealing the seeds of truth that God wants to plant. You might keep a notebook just for such impressions or jot them down in your daily journal. God may show you something, and if you don't write it down or make some kind of record that you can refer back to, it's way too easy to forget what he showed you.

I can't tell you how many times this has happened to me. I'll be wrestling with something I don't understand and praying about it. "God, are you there? What's going on? What do you want me to do in this situation? What are you up to?"

Then I often feel like God shows me something, provides direction, or speaks to my heart. I've learned to write it down, because inevitably, a few days later, I'll be thinking about it again, and I might talk myself out of it. "Well, I don't know. Maybe it was that late-night snack. Just some divinely inspired indigestion." So I begin to doubt what I knew with certainty only a couple of days ago. My awareness of God's message to me seems to vanish unless I write it down.

When I record it, though, it becomes a spiritual anchor that tethers me to God and to the consistency of his promises. "Yes, I believe that God has spoken." And better than that, I have a reference point that I can return to; it doesn't depend on my mood or what I had to eat the night before.

When you develop the discipline of writing down what God shows you and what you're praying about, you might be shocked over a few years at all that God does. George Mueller was a well-known evangelist who lived in the 1800s. One day, his heart broke when he saw hundreds of homeless children fending for themselves on the streets of Bristol in England.

With almost no money to his name, he decided to start an orphanage, and over the next sixty years, Mr. Mueller helped care for more than ten thousand orphans. All throughout his ministry, he kept a record of his prayers, in a journal that ultimately filled more than three thousand pages. He recorded how one night there was no food to give the children the next morning at breakfast, so he begged God to do something. Early the next morning, a local baker knocked at his door. When Mueller answered, the baker told him he hadn't been able to sleep the night before, so he had gotten up and baked three batches of bread, which he had brought for them. Another time, a milk truck just "happened" to break down in front of the orphanage on the exact day they had no milk for the children. Since the milk would have spoiled in the heat, the driver gave it to the orphans. All in all, Mr. Mueller recorded more than thirty thousand direct answers to his prayers. Just imagine how this built his faith, as he saw God's faithfulness laid out before him again and again in black and white.

If you are anything like me, journaling is a challenge. I can't count how many years I committed to journal daily, only to forget and quit by the middle of January. Finally, several years ago, I had a breakthrough. Someone gave me a five-year journal that has helped my relationship with God more than I can describe. Instead of pressuring me to write a couple pages a day about my feelings, prayer requests, and important events, this journal is way more simple. Each page represents one day but will eventually cover five years. For example, on January 1, there are five lines to write on for the current year. Then just below those five lines are five more lines, for January 1 next year. And so on. So essentially you are writing only a fifth of a page each day. And over a five-year period, you get to see what happened each year on that same day. The best part for me? Instead of writing pages, I have only a few lines to fill in, making it easy to continue.

During the first year, I found it easy and somewhat mean-ingful. The daily discipline helped me keep God at the front of my mind as I recorded something I was praying about each day.

But during year 2, I noticed something that really impacted me. When I returned to the same day from the previous year to begin the next one, suddenly I realized how many things that had weighed on me then were completely handled now. Problems worked out. Challenges met. Prayers answered. Concern with one of my kids had been resolved and was no longer even on my radar. Losing a valuable staff member had seemed like a big setback, but a year later we had someone in place who was even more effective. A challenge with a friendship had course-corrected, and we're closer now than ever before.

Journaling daily with a glimpse back to the previous year helped me see a bigger picture. Once I stopped obsessing over my present problems and started looking back to past ones, I could see how God was faithful in ways I might have missed otherwise. And the power of this realization came from one simple discipline: writing it down.

MAYBE YOU'RE THINKING, "COME ON, CRAIG! I GET WHAT YOU'RE saying, but I'm just not much of a writer. It's a great idea, but do you really expect me to get on my laptop—or even crazier, take out paper and pen—and write down what I think God is saying to me?"

Yes.

Absolutely.

You got it.

If you're serious about making it to the other side of this valley you're in, then you will want to talk to God, listen to what he says, and record what you believe he's showing you. Make your conversation with him tangible. The very act of putting words on the page or screen produces a testimony, seals a memory, and helps hold you accountable. Record his message to you.

Maybe you think God is telling you to trust him. Or to believe he has something different, maybe even something better. Or perhaps you sense he's leading you to do something about the problem yourself. Maybe you believe he's using this trial to change something inside you. To teach you patience. To teach you to trust. To build your faith. His delay is not his denial. As with the persistent widow in Luke 18, he wants you to keep believing and continue asking.

Write it down.

Another benefit of writing down what you think God is telling you is that you'll grow in discernment. Sometimes you really did just eat too much pizza the night before. Without going into all the details about how you can learn to listen when God is speaking to you, let me just remind you of three things. You can apply these simple suggestions to what you write down to help you discern whether they really are from God.

First, remember that God speaks to each of us in different ways. Rarely is it some audible voice booming out of the sky; usually it's a gentle whisper that wells up inside you, the voice of his Holy Spirit inside your heart. God can also speak through people. He might use your pastor, one of your parents, or a close friend to share his wisdom with you. God can also use circumstances to guide you, to slow you, or to redirect you toward his plan. And of course, God speaks through his Word, convicting, guiding, and comforting you. But you have to stop and listen. Tune out the distractions. Turn off your phone. Get alone in a quiet spot. And listen. Again, listening to God requires making time and space so you can hear him. And when you do hear from him, *write it down*. In fact, God might be showing you something right now, even as you're reading this book. Write it down in the margins, or take out a notebook and jot down what he's saying to you.

Second, God usually provides confirmation. Years ago, God gave me a vision for using technology to preach to more people in different locations. I was pretty sure this idea came from God, but when half of my church team had the same idea at the same time, that really confirmed it, for all of us. God may speak to you through other people, through events, by his Spirit, and through his Word. Often, depending on the emphasis of the message, these will even overlap. An idea springs up inside you, and you wonder if it's from God. Then the sermon that week directly addresses your idea, with Scripture to back it up. Then two friends who don't even know each other contact you, each wanting to talk about the same idea. When something like that happens, I would suggest that you listen.

Third, the messages we receive from God will always reflect his character; they'll be consistent with his Word. A loving and holy Father will not ask you to commit evil acts or to deliberately hurt others in his name. While sometimes the truth may hurt when we share it with someone, our job is to love them with that truth, not to condemn them with it. Nothing is too low for our Enemy. He often tries to counterfeit God's message. But the Lord is not a God of confusion. If he wants to tell us something—and we're willing to truly listen—his message will get through.

When you write down what God tells you, you can use it not only as an anchor but also as a litmus test. Every time you refer to it, you can compare it with what you see happening around you, and it can help guide you in your decisions. Be patient, and be consistent. It may take years before what he tells you comes to pass, as it did with the vision we had for our church. But if God makes you a promise, it will happen.

It's simply a matter of when.

2.3

Wait

Teach us, O Lord, the disciplines of patience,
for to wait is often harder than to work.
—Peter Marshall

With 4G technology for our smartphones, nanosecond internet access, and same-day delivery service from many major retailers, it's harder than ever to wait. Most of us don't have to wait very long for anything anymore. Just think about how antsy you feel when the dentist is running behind schedule and you're forced to play three more games of whatever you're playing on your mobile device. Drives you crazy, doesn't it?

Apparently, Habakkuk wasn't crazy about waiting either. Nonetheless, he knew that was the third thing he had to do if he was going to make it out of the valley of despondency. God told him, "The revelation awaits an appointed time; it speaks of the end and will not prove false. Though it linger, wait for it; it will certainly come and will not delay" (Hab. 2:3).

The Hebrew word here for "appointed time" is *mow'ed*, which means the right time, the affixed time, the divinely chosen time that God permits something to happen. There's an old saying that God is rarely early, never late, and always right on time. That's summed up by *mow'ed*.

When a woman is pregnant, she carries the child for about nine months, until her *mow'ed* for giving birth. And believe me, when it's time for that baby to come, it's time, and nothing is going to hold it back. I know firsthand. When Anna, our third child, was born, we were waiting for the obstetrician to arrive when Amy looked at me between contractions and said, "The baby's coming!"

I thought I should reassure her to just hang on. "I know, honey."

"No," she gasped. "I mean the baby is coming *right now!*"

Sure enough, I had to deliver our daughter. Her head came out, so I cradled it, and then the next thing I knew, I was diving low to catch her like a ground ball. I'd pat myself on the back as a hero, but right as she was coming out, I panicked and dropped her on the bed. Granted, it was only about a two-inch drop. But I couldn't take the pressure, and I let go. Part of me was proud that I didn't pass out. But the other part will never live down dropping my daughter.

It was just her time. There was nothing I could do to delay her arrival until the doctor could get there. When it's the *mow'ed*, there's nothing you or anyone else can do to speed it up or slow it down. It's going to happen, and happen on God's timetable.

Until then there's nothing you can do but wait and be ready.

WHEN GOD PROMISES YOU SOMETHING IN HIS WORD OR OTHER-wise, you may have to wait a while, but you can take his promises to the bank. Right now, you may know that you're in the waiting zone. You asked God what was going on, you listened for him, you made a record of what he said, and you believe God has shown you something. And now you're waiting and you're waiting and you're waiting and you're waiting. Maybe you're starting to fear that it won't come to pass.

Maybe you've been praying for what seems like forever for someone you love to come to Christ. But the harder you pray, the farther they seem to wander from God. So you wait. You might be asking God for another kind of miracle. For someone to be healed. For someone to be freed from an addiction. For a promotion. Or a spouse. So you pray. You wait. Then you wait some more. Perhaps you're brokenhearted about a rebellious child. You've done everything you know to do to help bring them back. You've read books. You've threatened. You've shown grace. And you've believed until you don't know if you can believe anymore. So you do more of what you've already been doing:

You wait.

When you feel like your faith tank is about to run dry, remember this: When God has promised something, it will come to pass. But it will be *his* timing, not yours. For whatever it's worth, you're not alone. Part of every believer's maturity involves waiting on God and waiting for his promises to be fulfilled. When you look through Scripture, you'll see example after example after example of people who are chosen by God, close to him, who still find themselves waiting. God promised them something, but then they had to wait for it. Let's look at just a few of them.

God told Moses, "I'm going to use you to deliver my people and rebuild the nation of Israel." Then Moses went on a forty-year road trip. Forty years! So much happened so fast with the exodus from Egypt—plagues and the first Passover and rushing out the door and strolling through the middle of the Red Sea before it closed up and drowned Pharaoh's army.

But then, after such a dramatic exit—and after many generations of slavery in Egypt, almost four hundred years—it wasn't surprising that the Israelites were eager to get to their new home. They probably thought it would take them a while to get there. A few weeks. Maybe a month or two. But forty years? That's how long it took, but God kept his promise. He led them to the promised land.

Or how about Joseph? You know, the guy with the rainbow coat? God told him, "You're going to be a great leader, over all your brothers and the entire nation." So what happens? His brothers throw him into a pit. Sell him into slavery. And then Joseph, falsely accused by his master's wife, is sent to prison. It was years before God finally fulfilled the promise, elevating him to second in command over all of Egypt. That's a long time to wait.

Now, here's one of my favorites. The apostle Paul has a vision and meets Christ. He's transformed and says, "I'm called to preach. That's what I'm here to do. This is all. I am compelled to preach the gospel. This is my God-given, singular purpose in life." And then he waits. Thirteen years pass before that purpose begins. Thirteen years before he gets to preach his very first message!

Some seasons in life, you just wait.

What do you do while you're waiting? A lot of people think of it like being in traffic or being in line at the grocery store. "Okay, I'm stuck here. I'm just going to have to wait this out. There's nothing I can do."

But the truth is, there's plenty to do!

What does a waiter do? They *wait* on customers who need to be served a meal. We should do the same thing. When we're waiting, we should be serving God the entire time. We're not just sitting around, waiting for something to happen.

Waiting on him doesn't mean there's no movement. In fact, there may be more movement when you're waiting than ever before.

The Bible tells us, "Whatever you do, whether in word or deed, do it all in the name of the Lord Jesus" (Col. 3:17). So even when we don't understand what God is up to and why we're having to go through the valley we're in, we continue to serve him and do what we know needs doing as we wait. I know: that's harder than it sounds, *especially* when you're drowning in a wellspring of hard times and painful emotions.

And that's where faith comes in.

2.4

By Faith

*Take the first step in faith. You don't have to
see the whole staircase, just take the first step.*
—Martin Luther King Jr

When it comes to faith, there's going to be waiting involved. I really like the way the Living Bible renders God's assurance to Habakkuk: "These things I plan won't happen right away. Slowly, steadily, surely, the time approaches when the vision will be fulfilled. If it seems slow, do not despair, for these things will surely come to pass. Just be patient! They will not be overdue a single day!" (Hab. 2:3 TLB). It's comforting to know that God's timing is perfect. I love the way C. S. Lewis put it: "I am sure that God keeps no one waiting unless he sees that it's good for him to wait." We can trust God to do what's best for us at the right time.

When I was growing up, whenever I got in trouble—especially if it was something my mom discovered I'd done that I shouldn't have—there were six little words that struck terror into my heart:

"Wait till your father gets home!" Depending on the severity of the crime, she might emphasize a different word: "*Wait* till your father gets home!" or "Wait till your *father* gets home."

My dad was a great and loving dad. He never did anything to hurt me, and he always had my best interests at heart when he disciplined me. But, as with most kids, hearing those fateful words always stopped me in my tracks. This meant it wasn't an "I did something wrong and Mom's gonna handle it" mistake. This wrong fell into "Dad will have to handle this one" territory. I'd think, "Uh-oh. I'd better start praying right now!" Then Dad would come home, he'd talk it over with Mom, then with me, and then he'd handle it. The anticipation was always worse than any punishment or consequences.

I suspect God used a tone similar to my mom's when he told Habakkuk to wait. Basically, God told his prophet, "I understand that the Babylonians are bad and you think they deserve some kind of punishment. Well, don't you worry, Habakkuk— they're going to get theirs. And it's going to be good. Just you wait. I'm the heavenly Father. I'm just and righteous, and they will face punishment for their sins." There's a sense of God asking Habakkuk to trust him and rest in the assurance that he will indeed make sure that justice prevails and that evil is thwarted. But it wasn't going to happen right away.

NOT ONLY DOES GOD PROMISE TO PUNISH THE BABYLONIANS, but he also makes it very clear why they will experience *his* punishment. These enemy invaders were puffed up and incredibly arrogant. "We don't need to follow God's rules. We're stronger than that. We've got it all together. We've got things figured out." The Babylonians saw themselves as the exception to God's rules. "Those laws are fine for the Israelites, but we do what we want."

So God cataloged some of their major offenses and described how they would be punished. Addressing the Babylonians who were thieves, he proclaimed, "Woe to him who piles up stolen goods" (Hab. 2:6). You are going to pay for what you have done. Next, he calls out the cheaters and deceivers: "Woe to him who builds his house by unjust gain" (v. 9). You are going to get what's coming to you. Those committed to violence didn't escape his notice, either: "Woe to him who builds a city with bloodshed" (v. 12). And finally, in his list of woes, God even pinpoints the partyers—yes, the partyers, the one "who gives drink to his neighbors" (v. 15)—and the idolaters (vv. 18–19).

I'm guessing that God's naming of the Babylonians' crimes and offenses had to bolster Habakkuk's faith. God made it clear that he knew *exactly* what was going on. He hadn't been looking the other way. He hadn't been preoccupied elsewhere. In fact, he had already decided *exactly* how he was going to punish them when the *mow'ed* came.

Oh, yeah . . . you just wait till your Father gets home.

EVEN WHEN WE'RE FORCED TO WAIT, GOD OFTEN REINFORCES his promises to us and reminds us of his presence. It might be through his Word, by a whisper, through a person, or simply through our believing by faith that he is with us. He makes it clear that he is not overlooking us or our needs. In return, he asks that we live by faith, trusting him and serving him during our season of waiting.

Not long ago in our small group, our close friends Rob and Dahrenda opened up to the rest of us about a recent trial. Even though they're innocent, they're being sued by a distant relative. Through tears, Dahrenda explained how much God must want them to depend on him. She said, "We've done everything we know to do. Now all we can do is wait." She continued, wiping away the tears. "God so wants our attention and affection that he's allowing us to walk through this trial to teach us to depend on him."

I sat in awe watching their faith mature right before my eyes, like a rose gently unfolding its petals to bloom.

To be clear, this type of maturity doesn't happen in a moment. It's a process that is born out of time with God and is usually the result of learning to trust him through something difficult. This kind of maturity is never easy, but when we see it in others, it strengthens us more than we realize. In fact, if you really want to strengthen your faith, I know of no better place to look than the book of Hebrews. There, in chapter 11, we find the Faith Hall of Fame, a list of so many people who struggled, waited, lived by faith, and saw God's promises fulfilled. There we find people going through unbelievable things—seemingly impossible trials—and ultimately experiencing a new level of intimacy with God even as they witness more of his power.

By faith, Noah obeyed God and built an ark, saving his family.

By faith, Abraham and Sarah received the son God promised them, even though they were past the age of childbearing.

By faith, Joseph overcame betrayal, slavery, false accusations, and imprisonment to save the nation of Israel.

By faith, God's people left Egypt and walked through the Red Sea as it parted on either side of them.

By faith, the Israelites marched around the walls of Jericho, and the walls came tumbling down.

These weren't perfect people—far from it, in fact. They all had their struggles and doubts, their mistakes and infidelities, their flaws and their weaknesses, but they persevered in their faith and waited on God again and again.

By faith, you will get through this.

Think about it: if you had everything figured out, you wouldn't need faith. You could live simply by your understanding. By your logic, but not by faith. But when you don't understand something, that gives you the unique opportunity to deepen your faith. Oswald Chambers said, "Faith is deliberate confidence in the character of God whose ways you may not understand at the time."

Michelle and Jonathan are two of my favorite staff members I get to work with regularly at church. After a couple years of praying about adoption, they decided it was something they wanted to pursue. They saved money to cover the costs, began preparing a room in their home for a new child, and met with placement experts to help them find a child in need.

Though they were open to adopting a child of any age, they were excited to learn about a mom of two who was pregnant and had decided it would be best for her to give up her third child for adoption. This poor, overwhelmed mom was severely impoverished. She had battled with drug addictions, and she now had as many "baby daddies" to deal with as she had children. In our office, we celebrated what seemed to be an answer to our prayers for our friends.

And then, when the baby was born, the birth mom changed her mind. Jonathan and Michelle were devastated. They were sad not just for their loss but also because they were concerned that this beautiful child they already loved might be entering into circumstances that likely meant she would face a much more difficult life.

So this precious couple did what anyone else would. They cried and cried and then cried some more. When I saw them the following week, I was surprised by their spiritual resolve. After I had hugged them both, Michelle told me confidently that they knew God loved that little baby way more than they did. Of course they were still disappointed, but they were placing all of their faith and trust in God's sovereign plan.

I could sense a spiritual deepening in this young couple that was well beyond their years. They were simultaneously wrestling with their disappointment and embracing the goodness of God.

So when your marriage is falling apart and the people around you and your spouse keep saying things like, "It's just too hard; you might as well go ahead and get divorced," you dig deep and remember the vows you made, trusting God by faith that all things are possible with him. When your kids keep making wrong decisions and everyone else says, "Oh man, they're so messed up; there's no hope," you believe by faith that God is working in their lives to bring about good to those who love him and are called according to his purpose.

When God promises you a child even when you haven't been able to conceive, you believe by faith that God will bring it about. Maybe he'll choose to give you a child by birth; maybe he'll choose instead to give you one by adoption. No matter what he does, you continue to believe by faith. Maybe you don't have enough money left for the rest of the month, but you're being obedient to God's Word, and by faith you give your tithe to him, trusting him as your ultimate provider.

You listen. You write down what God is showing you. Then, as you wait, you continue to believe by faith.

Faith isn't faith until it's all you're holding on to. If you don't have anything left to grasp, you continue to reach toward God.

You press on, one step after another, day by day, even when things are going wrong, to live by faith. You don't stop. You don't quit. You don't go back.

You walk by faith.

2.5

"Faith Tested"

I am one of those who would rather sink
with faith than swim without it.
—Stanley Baldwin, British Prime
Minister, 1923–29, 1935–37

What if you're living by faith and yet you don't see God's promise to you fulfilled in your lifetime? Can you dare to believe he will *still* keep his promise, even if you don't get to see it during your time on earth? Is it possible that you might grow so intimate with God that you're able to keep loving and serving him despite your disappointment?

Habakkuk is a good teacher for us on this lesson, because it was not until the next generation that God kept his promise and punished the Babylonians.

That's a long time to wait.

But the Lord was still faithful.

He always is.

Habakkuk gives us three little words that we can cling to

when it appears that God has not delivered on what he promised. No matter what you might be going through, never let go of these words.

If you truly want to come out of the valley and grow closer to God, then here's what you hold tightly on to. If you want to be able to grow closer to God—no matter what—then these are the three words you need to remember on your journey toward intimacy and ultimate trust and faith in him:

"But the LORD . . ."

You'll find these words in Habakkuk 2:20, where the prophet, after acknowledging that he still doesn't like what's going on, says, *"But the LORD is in his holy Temple. Let all the earth be silent before him"* (NLT, emphasis mine).

EVEN THOUGH I'M UPSET, ANGRY, CONFUSED, FRUSTRATED, DIS-appointed, and impatient, I will remember who God is.

The Lord is still in charge.

And he is good.

He is righteous.

He is true.

He is faithful.

He is all-knowing, all-powerful, and ever present.

The world may seem upside down, but the Lord is still there.

He is sovereign, and he has a plan—a much bigger plan than I can see right now.

I have to respect that he is God and I am not.

His timing is not my timing.

His ways are higher than I'll ever understand.

He is supreme in all wisdom, and he knows the end from the beginning.

I'm just a person, his creation.

He has everything under control.

SOMETIMES OUR FAITH IS TESTED UNTIL IT FEELS LIKE THERE'S hardly anything left. But here's amazing news: Jesus told us that even with just a speck of faith as tiny as a mustard seed, we can move mountains. If you want to believe, then you're pressing in with all your might toward knowing God and trusting him, even when your strength is nearly gone.

And what if *wanting* to believe is enough? What if that tiny bit of barely noticeable faith is still pleasing to God?

What if simply wanting to believe is the mustard seed of faith?

We see people who were put to the test in circumstances every bit as painful, and perhaps more personal, than Habakkuk's. Shadrach's, Meshach's, and Abednego's very lives were at stake. They faced a terrible dilemma, but in the end theirs was an easy choice. They said, "King Nebuchadnezzar is telling us to bow down and worship him instead of God, or he'll throw us in this fiery furnace. We're not going to bow down and worship a man, even if that man is a king. We believe that God will deliver us. We believe that God will rescue us. But even if he doesn't, it will still be okay. We're not bowing down to anyone but our Lord."

Do you see that deep, inward, unshakeable faith in a trustworthy God? Theirs wasn't a faith based on the outcome they desired; it was a faith based only on the character and goodness of God.

Essentially, these three teenagers stood boldly and declared,

"We believe our God can."
"We believe our God will."
"But even if he doesn't, we still believe."

How could they have such confidence? How could they be willing to die instead of take a lifesaving mulligan and then ask God for forgiveness later?

Because they believed that God had everything under control, and that was good enough for them.

They knew that even if they died a terrible, excruciating death in the flames of the king's furnace, God was still God. They believed that the Lord was on his throne and that they simply had to do their part and trust him.

And what about Job? Talk about seeing your whole life unravel! Job lost *everything*, but he could not make sense of why. His friends told him that he was obviously being punished, and yet Job couldn't think of anything he'd done to displease God—certainly not on such an extreme scale. His wife told him that he should just curse God and renounce the one who had clearly abandoned him. He refused. Instead he lived by faith. And he became even more intimate with God. Job said, "Though he slay me, yet will I hope in him" (Job 13:15). Nothing could strip Job's faith from him.

You might be shocked at how your trial can reveal a depth of faith you never knew you possessed. First Peter 1:7 says this: "These trials will show that your faith is genuine. It is being tested as fire tests and purifies gold—though your faith is far more precious than mere gold. So when your faith remains strong through many trials, it will bring you much praise and glory and honor on the day when Jesus Christ is revealed to the whole world" (NLT).

Habakkuk didn't get the answer he wanted from God, but still he believed. Although his life was about to grow even harder, still he chose to keep the faith. He knew that God was still God. He knew that God was still in charge. No matter what Habakkuk experienced, he kept coming back to those three little words that carry such enormous power:

"But the LORD . . ."

Extreme circumstances require extreme faith. Here is something I hope will be an encouragement to you: do you realize that just a tiny bit of faith is actually extreme faith?

Let me explain what I mean. There's a family in our church whose twenty-one-year-old daughter had a severe seizure. She'd had minor ones off and on for years, but this one was different: this time she didn't regain consciousness. Panicked, her family called for an ambulance. Unfortunately, Amy and I were out of the country when we got the news. It was several more days before we were finally able to get back and visit this family. And as each day passed, the news grew worse. First, the doctors said that she had brain damage. Next, they said that her brain was dead, which meant she wouldn't survive without life support. Finally, they recommended that the family start discussing when they should remove their daughter from life support.

When we walked into that room, the whole family just erupted with grief. With tears flowing freely and no words to say, we just sat there and held each other for what seemed like hours. Finally, the girl's mom asked if we would pray for their daughter. I had some ideas about what I should pray, but out of respect for the tenderness and sensitivity of such a desperate situation, I asked them how they would like me to pray. The mother—who was, well . . . let's just say she was not exactly the most involved and committed church attender—met my puffy eyes with her own. With just a hint of resolve, she said, "I know the experts say there is no hope, but I still want to believe that God could heal her."

And there it was, a seed of faith.

Not much. Barely noticeable. A seed.

So we prayed. And as best we could, we believed against all odds that this girl would be healed.

To be honest, this is the type of prayer that, as a pastor, I pray often. Many times, a few days later I end up performing the funeral of that same person. This time, things were different. Within days she started improving. Within weeks she went home. God had heard our prayer. And he did the impossible. The Lord was with that family.

I also spent time with another family, whose nineteen-year-old daughter, Bethany, had brain cancer. Her doctors were fairly confident that they had gotten all the cancer cells during her two surgeries. They projected that Bethany had many years left to live. Tragically, about nine months later she died suddenly. The cancer had returned with a vengeance.

Some might ask why God was with the first family and not with the second. I hope you can see that God was with them both—simply in different ways. For the first family, God was with them as healer. For the second, he was with them as comforter. Though they experienced one of life's deepest losses, they also experienced one of life's deepest measures of God's grace. He was there for them every moment of every painful day.

His grace was enough.

When you have nowhere else to turn, when your own ideas and resources have evaporated, when your control over a situation is in shambles, God is still there. When your knees ache from kneeling in prayer but you can't tell if he's even listening, God is still there. When people laugh at you, mocking you for your faith, God is still there. When you don't know if you can make it another day, God is still there. When the voice of your Enemy is whispering to you that you should just give up, God is still there.

He loves you. He is for you. He will never leave you nor forsake you. He will never let you down. He may not do exactly what you want. But he is always faithful, no matter how much your circumstances may seem to indicate otherwise.

No matter what happens in your life, the Lord is in his holy temple.

PART 3

Hope and Glory

3.1

Remember

If you think God has forgotten you,
then you have forgotten who God is.
—Anonymous

Recently I was on the phone making some changes to our bank account. To verify my identity, the customer service person asked me for the PIN on the account. I told her what I thought it was, but evidently I gave her the wrong one. When had it changed?

So then she wanted to know not only the last four digits of my Social Security number but also the addresses of two of our previous homes and the name of my favorite childhood pet (which, in case you're wondering, was not a cat).

Thankfully, I was able to remember all of those things, even though many of them were from ten, fifteen, even twenty years ago or more. I marvel at how amazing the human mind is—especially its ability to record and store data in the form of memory. Because this subject is intriguing to me, I did a little research online, reading about the differences between short-term and long-term memory. There are essentially two things that distinguish these two types from one another. The first is the significance that we attach to the thing we're remembering. The second is how frequently we think about it—how often we recall that memory or how frequently it springs to mind on its own.

Obviously, important things like your Social Security number and the addresses of places where you live for a long time embed somewhere in your long-term memory. But PINs and computer passwords, which often change every few months, can be more slippery. Because our minds are constantly aware that the significance of such things is limited, we keep track of them only on the surface of our memory. For most of us, there's an expiration date on those kinds of details. That's why we seldom retain specific moments from our daily routines in long-term memory; they have to be really good or really bad, or stand out somehow from the usual.

That's why I can vividly remember the amazing steak dinner Amy lovingly prepared for our anniversary, but I can't tell you what I ate for dinner last night. It's why I remember what my kids wrote on my last Father's Day card but not what came in the mail yesterday. It's why I remember how hard it was to get through a season when Amy was really sick but not the last time I had a cold.

We remember what matters most to us, because we replay it often in our memory.

I SHARE MY LITTLE STROLL DOWN MEMORY LANE BECAUSE ONE of the best aids to climbing out of the valley is remembering what God has done for us. Not just what he has done for people in the Bible, for the nation of Israel, for our parents or our friends, or even for our church but what he's done for *me*.

Habakkuk understood this. In the third and final chapter of his book, we find his prayer, which we're told is "on *shigionoth*." While scholars don't know exactly what *shigionoth* means, it's likely a musical or literary form. So basically, Habakkuk chose a specific artistic structure or setting in which to share his prayer. Even though we don't know the precise form, it strikes me that the same guy who was asking God some rather accusing questions has now changed his tune. We see this same kind of movement—from doubt to faith—in the Psalms. It's similar to singing a worship song that acknowledges how hard life is and yet how much we can trust God. It's another step, a really big one, in the journey out of the valley.

But climbing out of the valley is not just trying to go through the motions and putting on a happy face when you're really hurting and troubled. People tell me sometimes that they can't come to church and sing upbeat, feel-good worship songs when they're suffering through a financial crisis or their child's addiction or the results of a medical test. I tell them that's okay, they can still worship God from wherever they are; we all can.

Habakkuk prays, "LORD, I have heard of your fame; I stand in awe of your deeds, LORD. Repeat them in our day, in our time make them known; in wrath remember mercy" (Hab. 3:2).

There's a respectful, appreciative tone to the way he begins here. It's as if he were saying, "Well, if I'm honest, God, I've seen past seasons in which your presence seemed more real than now. You were doing big things then. And I know that's the kind of God you are. But please do those same kinds of things again, for us now. Repeat all those great feats that I know you've done before." In fact, the Hebrew word that's translated "repeat" here is *chayah*, which simply means to renew, to revive, or restore.

From there, Habakkuk's prayer lists some very tangible and visible places and events that will trigger spiritual memories for God's people. He lists specific locations: Teman, Mount Paran, Cushan, and Midian. He also mentions several of God's creations: ancient mountains, rivers and streams, heavens and earth, sun and moon. These verses may not have the same effect on us as they did on the people in Habakkuk's day. But the call to remember what God has done remains timeless, even for us.

While certainly we could research and appreciate the historical events that Habakkuk references (and I would recommend that you do sometime), his prayer basically challenges us to recall our own key memories: those people, places, moments in time, and provisions that reveal the bigger picture of God's presence in our lives. Habakkuk urges us to draw on our long-term memories of God rather than being so shortsighted that we choose to keep replaying only our immediate, distressing circumstances.

That's a funny thing about memory. Scientists tell us that one of the most powerful ways we can recall events from the past is through what they call "sense memory." In fact, many studies have suggested that smells may be the most powerful sense memory of all. That's certainly true for me. There's this perfume that Amy wore when we first met, and every time I smell it now, I think of . . . well, I think of our six kids, if you know what I mean.

Maybe when you smell the tantalizing aroma of an apple pie baking, you remember your grandma's house or a special dinner your mom used to make. Songs can have a similar effect, taking us right back to a specific time and place in our lives. If you're around my age, every time you hear Air Supply, Lionel Richie, or Chicago, you remember your first couples skate or your junior prom. (And if you're way younger than I am, you're probably wondering why someone would need an Air Supply, who Lionel Richie is, and what was he doing in Chicago?)

For the people of Israel, when Habakkuk mentions the names of these places, memories of the things that happened there leap to mind. Teman and Mount Paran refer to the places where the Israelites took refuge after God delivered them from Egyptian bondage. Suddenly the people can feel their hearts racing as they remember dashing out the door with just the clothes on their backs, believing that freedom was no longer a dream but a real possibility. They can smell the Red Sea and recall the sight of those huge walls of water closing behind them once they had all made it across. It's almost as if Habakkuk were saying, "Hey, guys, remember when . . ." and the Israelites all share those memories of what God did for them.

It's that experience we have with children when we read them a story or do a silly voice or magically pull a quarter out of their ear. How do they always respond? "Do it again, Daddy! Do it again!" After we were engaged, I gave Amy a children's book called *Miffy's Bicycle*. She looked at me funny at first, but then I explained that I looked forward to reading it to our kids someday. Well, sure enough, six kids later, I've read that book so many times that the pages are falling out. Night after night, the kids would beg me, "Read it again, Daddy! And tell me the part about how you gave this to Mommy even before I was born!"

Our kids love this story, partly because they instinctively know that it connects them to history, to their origins, their family, where they came from. Habakkuk understood the power of this kind of remembering. He paints a vivid picture of God displaying his glory and power through nature—helping the people remember.

I can almost imagine him saying, "God, I remember what you did. You stunned us all with your power and glory. I remember when you guided your people by fire and by cloud. I remember when you fed us with bread from heaven. I remember when the waters parted and we walked through on dry land. I remember when you shook the earth and the walls came tumbling down. I remember when you used torrential rains to defeat people who wanted to harm us. I remember when you sent pestilence and plagues against our enemies. God, I remember what you can do. Now please renew those deeds in our day."

WHEN I'M IN THE VALLEY, SOMETIMES I SIMPLY NEED TO REMEM-
ber. I just have to recall all that God has done in my life—for
me, through me, even in spite of me. I return to who I know
God is. When I can't see him in my present situation, I remember what he's done in the past.

I remember when I was in college and more lost than you
could ever imagine, and I called out to Jesus, asking him—no,
almost daring him, "*If* you're real, and if you *are* there, *do*
something." What he did was so supernatural, I will never
forget that moment as long as I live. I fell down on my knees
as one person, I met him there in prayer, and then when I
stood up, I was a completely different person. I savor that
moment.

And then I remember how God brought Amy into my life.
It remains a miracle of miracles that I get to spend the rest of
my life with my best friend and my spiritual partner and the
mother of my half dozen awesome kids. I cherish her and the
gift she was and continues to be from God.

And then I remember when our daughter Catie was born,
and how as a little girl she was just so in love with Jesus.
I remember how, when she was about three years old, Catie
got into some poison ivy and ended up covered in a rash from
head to toe. Before bed that night, she told me, "Daddy, Jesus
is going to heal me because I prayed." I remember thinking,
"Wow, that's really sweet. But I don't know what we're going
to do if she still has this rash tomorrow." I remember that the
next morning, Catie came running into our room, buck naked
and giddy with joy, shouting, "Look! Look! He healed me!"

And that rash. Was. Completely. Gone. I marvel at that moment and the way God heard the prayer of a child.

I remember when Amy and I were young, just starting out in ministry, and we didn't have any money. We prayed together, "God, we don't know where food's coming from tomorrow." The next day, we received a refund check in the mail. We felt that God understood what we were going through, that he cared, and that he provided. We still feel that way.

I remember when we started the church, and we had just moved into a new location in a grade school cafeteria. I stood up one Sunday in front of about a hundred people and told them matter-of-factly, "The school said we can't meet here anymore. I don't know where we're going to go, but I believe that God will provide." And I remember that on Thursday of that same week, someone let us move into their building, a little bike factory, and we were knocking out the walls and rearranging the space because God had provided.

I remember building our first building. And I remember when it started filling up four times on the weekend, and we didn't have enough money to build again. I remember what it was like when we had to turn away people because we didn't have enough room for them. I remember praying, "God, please give us a miracle gift." And then another church nearby called and asked, "Could we merge churches with you?" Thirty days later their members voted to give us their debt-free building and join in what we were doing. I remember that day felt to me as miraculous as Pentecost must have felt for those first-century believers.

I remember the time I went to visit someone in the hospital.

Her family told me, "They've said she has less than an hour to live," and everyone gathered to say their goodbyes. I remember that we prayed and, as we did, immediately her vitals began to change. Two days later this lady went home, healed.

I remember the time I was talking with a couple after church, and through tears they told me, "For seven years we've tried everything, but we just can't have a baby. Would you pray for us?" I prayed, and something happened during that prayer that had never happened before and hasn't happened since. I couldn't even tell you why I would say this, but after that prayer I told them, "Decorate your kid's room. And make it blue, because nine months from now God's going to give you a son." Nine months later they welcomed their baby boy.

Regardless of where you are in your relationship with God right now, you have them too: those memories of when he was clearly involved in your life. You might think your examples aren't as important as the examples I just shared. Remember: every time God acts and reveals himself, it's important. He is constantly showing us that he is with us and that he cares. Maybe it was the time when you were hurting so badly and then turned on the radio and heard a song that sounded like it was God's message especially to you in that moment. Or it could have been something as simple as that day you were reading the Bible and came across a verse and thought, "Oh, my goodness! If this verse was ever for anyone, it must be for me." Or when you were down and feeling alone, and a friend called and said, "Sorry if this seems odd, but God put you on my heart, and I really felt like I should call you."

What do you do when you're in the valley?

You remember what God has done. When he comforted you. When he guided you. When he answered your prayer exactly the way you wanted him to. And when he didn't do what you wanted, but sometime later you realized it was exactly what you needed.

And you dare to believe that what he's done before, he will do again.

3.2

Accept

It's not denial. I'm just selective
about the reality I accept.
—Bill Watterson, *Calvin and Hobbes*

Several years ago, when our kids were still young, they experienced their first crisis of belief. Even though I'm not a big fan of cats, we've always had them. Why? Because my kids love them. And I love my kids even more than I dislike cats. Anyway, back then we had two cats, Cutie Pie and Pumpkin, and the kids really loved them.

One night as we were pulling into our driveway, we saw a bobcat sprint across our yard. It was a pretty wild experience; the kids were really excited, like we'd just seen Bigfoot or something. But the bobcat sighting took on a different tone the following morning when Pumpkin didn't show up for breakfast.

For five years, Pumpkin had always been right on the porch first thing in the morning, meowing and ready to eat.

So when she didn't show up that morning, I couldn't help but wonder if that bobcat had a little Pumpkin muffin of his own for breakfast. I didn't want to say anything, but after the second morning and still no Pumpkin, the kids started worrying and asking questions. And then they started praying.

Our boys were about five and seven at the time, and Joy was three. They all looked so serious and sad, and they started asking me tough questions. "Daddy, uh, Pumpkin is coming home, right? Right, Dad? Right? 'Cause we've been praying and praying for her to come back. So she'll come home, won't she? Because God wouldn't let anything happen to our cat. Right?"

"Well, I sure hope Pumpkin comes home," I said, not sharing my suspicion about her fate. Like any good parent, I put up lost cat signs in our neighborhood, called animal shelters nearby, and asked around to see if anyone had seen Pumpkin. With each sign we put up, the kids' confidence level grew. They just knew that God was going to bring their cat back.

After almost a week, I had to sit down with them and say, "Listen, guys. I'm really, really sorry, but I don't think Pumpkin's coming back." It was a tender, sweet, challenging moment. And these little bitty kids with their precious, earnest faith wanted answers. "But, Daddy . . . we prayed. Why didn't God bring our cat home?" So I had to explain to them that sometimes God does things that we don't understand. Maybe even things that hurt us, disappoint us, and baffle us. And we just have to accept it when that's what he chooses.

SOMETIMES, EVEN WHEN WE REMEMBER ALL THAT GOD HAS done for us, it doesn't change our circumstances. Sometimes we just have to accept that it's beyond our understanding right now and just keep going. But we must also realize that acceptance is not denying the reality of what we're experiencing and how we feel about it. It simply means acknowledging the truth of the situation, expressing our feelings, and looking to God for what he's going to do.

Acceptance is not denial. When you accept what God is doing, you don't simply stuff your feelings down and let your heart die, even as you're practicing your smile in the mirror and memorizing Bible verses. When you accept that God's up to something that you can't see or understand right now, you don't just roll over and play dead and resign yourself to despair. No, you keep praying for a miracle from him unless he tells you otherwise, as he did with Habakkuk. But you don't pretend that everything is okay when clearly it's not.

Unfortunately, too often I see struggling Christians trying to make their faith something separate that they have to endure, like a wool coat that's two sizes too small which they're forced to wear in July. They try to act like they're cool and calm when there's obviously no way they could be. I call these kinds of believers HITS Christians, because they've stuck their Heads In The Sand.

These people misuse their faith by putting on sand-colored glasses. When the doctor says, "Hey, your health's not very good. You need to make some changes. We need to watch your heart," they don't listen. Rather than facing the truth and accepting it, they just put their head in the sand. When their marriage is in trouble and their spouse says, "Look, we need counseling," they say things like, "I hear what you're saying, but for now let's just trust God and it'll all work out." They put their heads in the sand.

Sometimes when finances are bad, these people say, "But I want the house. I know God has promised me this house." So they risk everything and go into debt way beyond what they can afford. Even when every trusted friend advises against it, they buy the house "on faith." And they put their head in the sand. When the storm is coming, some Christians don't prepare for the reality—the inevitability—that it will hit. They don't face the truth. They just put their head in the sand, pretending we're all still in the garden of Eden.

Maybe God is trying to tell you something through your circumstances, something like, "Pull your head out—now!"

HABAKKUK CERTAINLY COULDN'T KEEP HIS HEAD IN THE SAND. After he questioned God and the Lord responded by telling him that he was going to use the wicked Babylonians to destroy Israel, Habakkuk said, "I heard and my heart pounded, my lips quivered at the sound; decay crept into my bones, and my legs trembled" (Hab. 3:16).

His response is visceral. You know that sinking sensation you get in your gut when something bad happens that's beyond your control? You know how your body tries to just absorb whatever you're going through, your muscles tense up and stiffen, and you get headaches and stomachaches? Well, imagine God telling you that he's going to use your nation's worst enemy to destroy you. That's what Habakkuk was facing. He looked truth squarely in the face and said, "This is not going to be a fun season. In fact, it's going to be awful. A lot of innocent people are going to die. Probably people I love. Probably me. There's going to be a lot of bloodshed. I don't like it, but I have to trust God, even though I don't fully understand."

It's not a denial. It's faith. Not faith that God will do what Habakkuk wants God to do. But faith in God's character. Habakkuk goes on to say, "The sovereign hand of God is doing something here. God has spoken, so I'll accept whatever he is doing, as difficult as that may be for me."

Sometime, something is going to happen that you don't like. It may be happening right now. Sometimes you just need more patience, sincere faith, deeper trust, even if your cat isn't coming home. So how do you pull yourself out of the valley?

You remember what God has done.

You accept what God is doing.

You trust what God is going to do.

3.3

Trust

The best proof of love is trust.
—Joyce Brothers

It was one of the hardest funerals I've ever attended, let alone tried to lead. Bill, a close friend and rock-solid member of our church, had died unexpectedly at age forty-six, leaving behind his wife and five kids. Our entire community grieved along with them. His family had asked me to preach at the funeral service, and of course I agreed.

I had no idea what to say or how to begin. Sure, I had plenty of sermons in a file from past funerals and memorial services, lots of Scripture passages, and yet none of that seemed right. Bill was such a good friend to our family, and I was grieving right along with everyone else—remembering conversations we'd had, the corny jokes he told, and the projects we'd worked on together.

So I stood at the podium to begin the service, and I still didn't know what to say. I started and hesitated. Paused. Surged with emotion. Tried to start again and couldn't. And then I felt like I knew what to say—what Bill would want me to say to begin his funeral. I took a deep breath, and by faith I said what felt almost impossible in the face of losing someone like him.

"God is good!"

There was a moment of silence as the entire room seemed to exhale, and then everyone responded together, "All the time!"

It was like a spiritual sigh of relief. In our deepest grief and confusion, together we acknowledged the continual goodness of God. Almost two decades later people still talk about that moment. It wasn't easy, but it demonstrated our willingness to keep trusting God despite the heavy sadness shrouding our hearts at that time.

Coming out of the dip and using our crisis of belief as a catalyst to reaching a higher, more intimate plateau with God requires trust. We have to make choices about what we believe is true, exercise our willpower to act on those beliefs, and yet remain honest about the way things appear to us and how we feel. If we allow any of those parts to override the others, then we'll usually end up sliding back down into the valley again.

Habakkuk offers us an amazing model of a healthy, balanced response to what had to be about the worst news he could have received from God. Even as his body reacted, he realized that he had a choice about what he was going to believe. He could trust his emotions. He could trust his current view of the situation. Or he could trust that God could somehow bring good out of an inconceivable scenario—the Babylonians invading their land.

Habakkuk prays, "I heard and my heart pounded, my lips

quivered at the sound; decay crept into my bones, and my legs trembled. Yet I will wait patiently for the day of calamity to come on the nation invading us. Though the fig tree does not bud and there are no grapes on the vines, though the olive crop fails and the fields produce no food, though there are no sheep in the pen and no cattle in the stalls, yet I will rejoice in the LORD, I will be joyful in God my Savior" (Hab. 3:16–18).

Even though he could barely stand after hearing the devastating news, even though things weren't heading in the direction he'd hoped, even though the hard time just got worse than he could have predicted, still he chose to rejoice in God's goodness. Just like all of us at Bill's funeral, Habakkuk grieved with a heavy heart, and yet he was still able to say, "God is good."

Basically, he chose to trust God more than any tangible, physical, concrete evidence that he might encounter. "Even though my body's a wreck, and even though all the fruit trees and crops fail, even though we have no livestock, I'm still going to rejoice in the Lord." Is that crazy or what?

YEARS AGO, A CHRISTIAN COUNSELOR FRIEND OF MINE AND I were talking one day about all the terrible, painful, unbelievable things that people go through. I had shared with him that often the hardest struggle for me is seeing babies born with life-threatening defects, children who become terminally ill, and young adults—talented, kind, God-loving teenagers—who die unexpectedly in a car crash or school shootings. My friend agreed that those were some of the hardest losses to face.

"So what do you tell people when they come to see you with that kind of intense, unbearable, unimaginable loss?" I asked.

He looked at me for a moment and then said quietly, "The truth."

I waited for him to continue.

"I tell them that I don't have any good reason for this. But that God grieves with them just as much and will somehow use this as a catalyst for a greater good."

We sat in the powerful silence of his statement for a moment.

"And you really believe that?" I asked. It wasn't that I doubted him; I just knew that my friend could not have said those words unless he had experienced some excruciating losses in his own life.

"I do," he said. "It took me a long time—years—but yes, I do."

He went on to share about having been abused in his childhood by a friend of his family, about his father's alcoholism, about his attempts to run away from God in college through drugs, sex, and alcohol.

"Sometimes," he concluded, "we have to grieve the losses in our life before we can clear a space inside, where our faith has room to grow. That's the only way to grow closer to God when terrible things happen."

In your life, it may feel like the Babylonians have already ravaged the landscape of your heart. You may be grieving losses that occurred years ago. But even in the middle of all that pain, if you can choose to trust God despite all kinds of evidence to the contrary, then you will break through to a new level of intimacy with him. You will know his presence in the middle of your hurting. You will trust his character when you don't understand your circumstances. Then, no matter what happens, no matter how painfully your heart is pierced, you can continue to take one more step for one more day.

As with Habakkuk, your prayer becomes honest about what you've lost or will lose, even as you realize that you still have God.

"Even though my spouse said till death do us part and didn't live up to their word, I will still rejoice in the Lord my God."

"Even though I raised my kids to know better and they're making very scary decisions right now, yet will I trust in the Lord my God."

"Even though we've prayed for someone's health to get better and they've gotten worse, yet I will trust in the Lord my God."

"Even though our house will not sell and we are on the line, I will yet trust in the Lord my God."

"Even though finances are tough and it's going to cost four hundred dollars to repair my car, yet I will trust in the Lord my God."

"Even though I don't like it, even though I don't understand it, even though I know he could and he should but he's not, yet will I trust in the Lord my God."

3.4

Hope

A living hope enables us to have both
sorrow and joy. Our living hope is an
inheritance achieved for us by Christ.
—Tim Keller

M any people have enjoyed watching and rewatching *The Shawshank Redemption*, the story of an innocent man convicted of killing his wife who was then sentenced to life behind bars. It's an inspiring movie, sort of a modern classic, and offers a powerful message about freedom, joy, and hope.

But imagine what it would be like to find yourself in a real-life situation in which you are wrongly accused and convicted of a crime you can't even imagine, let alone carry out. Imagine that you're charged with murdering not one, not two, but *six* people, including four children. Imagine that you receive the death penalty for these crimes that you did not commit. Imagine that you are given the date of your execution, not once but *twice*, with a stay coming both times just days before you are to be put to death. Imagine that you're in prison for years and years—eighteen in all—before anything changes.

Anthony Graves lived through this horrific ordeal. He was eventually exonerated and released after his case was reviewed by a law professor and her students with the Innocence Project, a group committed to overturning legal injustice in our country. His experiences would have driven even the most patient, faith-filled individual to despair. His case was mishandled at every level, and the Texas attorney general cited "egregious misconduct" by the prosecutor in his trial.

But if you talk to Anthony today or hear him speak about his experiences, you'll find that he's one of the most positive, inspiring, hope-filled people you could ever meet. His credibility is off the charts. Here's a man who suffered injustice on a grand scale, losing almost two decades of his life, along with his reputation. But throughout that time, Anthony never lost his faith. Oh, he definitely wrestled with God, once throwing his Bible at the wall in his cell after reading passages like the one in James 1 that says to count it all joy when we face trials.

But he quickly realized the truth of his situation. He was innocent. He and God (and of course the real killer) may have been the only ones who knew this, but Anthony became more confident each day that God had not abandoned him and would somehow bring something good—something he could not even imagine on his own—out of this terrible ordeal.

God kept his promise to Anthony Graves. Today Anthony speaks, blogs, and writes about prison reform, capital punishment, and our legal system. His story now impacts tens of thousands of people. His faith in Jesus and love of God are abundantly evident. He knows what it means to have hope when there's every reason to despair.

The same can be true for you.

HABAKKUK WASN'T IMPRISONED, BUT HE DID KNOW WHAT IT was like to feel confined by terrible circumstances. Nonetheless, as we have seen, he was still able to remember all that God had done for him, to accept that God was up to something more than meets the human eye, and to trust that God would bring about something glorious from the ruins of the present. Habakkuk concludes his prayer, "The Sovereign LORD is my strength; he makes my feet like the feet of a deer, he enables me to tread on the heights" (Hab. 3:19).

When you consider what this prophet knew he was already facing—and that it was about to get a lot worse when the Babylonians came to town—it's stunning that he can pray this prayer. "Even though the fig tree doesn't bud and there are no animals in the barn, yet the Lord is in his holy temple. Even though it's going to get worse before it gets better, be still all the earth before him. The righteous will live by faith. God's word will be true. I will find my strength and my hope in the Lord my God, and he will take me to new heights."

It's like my friend Jade, a guy I knew from a job I had during high school. Unfortunately, Jade backed himself into a corner with horrible, sinful decisions. After he cheated on his wife, not once but twice, she had had enough. Now that she's left him, Jade grieves his sins deeply and clearly recognizes how he got off track. Now he is back in fellowship with God, doing the right things, but his life is still in shambles. At this moment, there is no evidence that his life will ever improve the way we would all like to see. But he isn't giving up. When we talk, I remind him that God is with him. And each day, God's strength keeps him encouraged, carries him through the pain of his current condition. There is no miracle story yet: his marriage isn't restored; his kids are still angry. And he hasn't found some new purpose in life. But I know that I know that I know God will continue to sustain Jade daily and bring a new story of restoration that will unfold over time. Because the Lord is on his throne. And he is always faithful.

While you or I might feel like a squashed bug under the weight of Habakkuk's circumstances, he compares himself to a mountain deer, one with steady feet, about to climb the heights. One about to rise up out of the valley of despair, depression, and desolation and reach the mountaintop.

Faced with what seems unbearable, unbelievable, we can find no better response than Habakkuk's. If you take nothing else away from this little book, I hope you'll remember what Habakkuk's name means: To wrestle. And to embrace.

Sometimes we can't tell the difference.

I remember when my youngest daughter, Joy, was barely four years old and playing on a friend's backyard zip line. Since she was too small to keep herself from hitting the tree at the end of the line, she smashed her face square into its thick trunk.

I can still remember hearing that *crack!* and seeing blood all over her face. She fell to the ground, unconscious.

Panicked, I felt for a pulse. It was still there, although not as strong as I would have liked. We rushed her to the ER, and the doctors began running tests and doing everything they could to make sure she was okay. Once she regained consciousness, they tried to stitch up the gash on the bottom of her chin. But Joy wasn't having it. She squirmed and fought and screamed and fought some more.

So I had to pin her down.

I was lying on top of her, holding her body and head still while the doctor carefully dressed her cuts and stitched them up. It was awful. She was crying so hard, sobbing, "Daddy, what's going on? Please let go. Please. Make them stop. I want to play. Please. I just want to play. Please don't let them hurt me." But I knew that if she was going to heal properly, she had to go through this.

I'm convinced that so often we go through these times when we kick and scream and fight God, and all he's really trying to do is hold us and guide us through the storm. We want to ask questions and demand answers, to hold him accountable and to have him remedy the situation immediately. But he knows that's not possible—for our own good. Just as I knew that I had to hold Joy down if she was going to heal, sometimes God must envelop us in ways that feel rigid and confining.

To wrestle and to embrace.

Both at the same time.

3.5

Believe

I believe in Christianity as I believe that
the sun has risen: not only because I see it,
but because by it I see everything else.
—C. S. Lewis

Hope is a funny thing. When you truly trust God, you have something to look forward to, a kind of divine antici-pation for where he's taking you. You also have a security you can rest in, the certainty that no matter how bad things seem, he's still in control and on your side. And you have a desire for change—probably in your circumstances, but more important, in your heart. You want to be closer to God. When you add up all these things, you get the kind of hope that allows you to climb up beyond your present circumstances and confusion.

Proverbs tells us, "Hope deferred makes the heart sick, but a dream fulfilled is a tree of life" (13:12 NLT). The Proverbs also tell us, "Where there is no vision, the people perish" (29:18 KJV).

There's something about the power of hope that fuels us and enables us to persevere.

It's amazing what you can endure when you have a reason.

No one illustrated this better than Jesus. When he knelt in the garden of Gethsemane, he knew what he would have to endure. The beatings. The scourging. The mocking. The torture. The humiliation.

But Jesus continued moving forward. He remained faithful to his Father.

How did Jesus do it? The writer of the book of Hebrews gives us a glimpse. Hebrews 12:2–3 says, *"For the joy set before him* he endured the cross, scorning its shame, and sat down at the right hand of the throne of God. Consider him who endured such opposition from sinners, so that you will not grow weary and lose heart"* (emphasis mine). Jesus just needed one reason to press through the pain. One good reason to stay. What was his reason? It was the "joy set before him."

You were the reason he came.

You were the joy set before him.

If you don't even know where you're going, what's the point of continuing to press forward? Without hope, it's hard to get out of the valley and stay out.

What are you looking forward to right now, today? Maybe it's the ham and Swiss sandwich on rye bread that you're going to have for lunch. Meeting your friend after work for a double espresso at your favorite coffee shop. Attending that party at your sister's house this weekend. Going to the beach for vacation next summer. Seeing the expression on your child's face when they open the present you just bought them. Getting your annual bonus.

There's nothing wrong with looking forward to any of these. But usually the things we look forward to and antici- pate, the things we hope for, are short-term moments of gratification. After all, we can have virtually anything we want sooner than almost any other people in history. Fresh peaches, even during the subzero temperatures of January? No problem. A car loan despite your dismal credit rating? Lots of places will be happy to help you. Ask your phone to give you turn-by-turn directions to the party, and your phone talks back to you!

But usually, the things that mean the most require time. Building loving relationships. Trusting someone. Watching your kids grow up. Finding a fulfilling job. Sure, the little things might get us through the day, the week, the month.

But only the hope of the Lord can get us through life.

TRUE HOPE BOTH REQUIRES AND RELIES ON SECURITY, A FIRM foundation in the power that is the basis for that hope. As the author of Hebrews explains, leading into that Faith Hall of Fame that we walked through in part 2, "Faith is the substance of things hoped for, the evidence of things not seen" (Heb. 11:1 KJV). But we all know how hard it can be to exercise our faith when we can't see any concrete reason to base it on. So by its very definition, it seems like faith is doing something for which you have no logical basis. And without the character of

God—and our relationship with him—as our foundation, we might as well be hoping in Santa Claus or our iPhone.

No matter what we see and feel, God is more real than anything else in our lives. And I realize that all of these abstract ideas and concepts can start to seem confusing or feel detached from the flesh-and-blood, bills-and-bankruptcy trials you may be going through. But they *do* matter, and Scripture explains their relationship this way: "We also glory in our sufferings, because we know that suffering produces perseverance; perseverance, character; and character, hope. And hope does not put us to shame, because God's love has been poured out into our hearts through the Holy Spirit, who has been given to us" (Rom. 5:3–5).

Here's my take on this progression from suffering to intimacy with God: When we're suffering through hard times, we take God at his Word and believe that he's still in control, with a specific purpose in mind. So we keep going, relying on him. As we keep going, hour to hour, day to day, week to week, we become stronger. Our faith grows, our maturity grows, our trust in God grows. When we're stronger, then our hope is in God's goodness, not in our circumstances. We learn not to trust in our senses but to trust in God's promises.

If you still want to believe, then God will meet you in the midst of your efforts to believe. Even if you throw your Bible across the room, as Anthony Graves did, or shake your fist at God or question him, as Habakkuk did, God will honor the passionate sincerity of your pursuit. If you really want to experience God's closeness and care for you as you go through trials—and you desire that more than you hope your circumstances will change and your comfort will return—then he will come alongside you with each and every step.

THIS JOURNEY OF FAITH IS EASIER SAID THAN DONE, I KNOW. And so often, as we've seen, it's a matter of perspective. Just to emphasize this point, I have a little poem that I think will help you. These verses were written by a young man from our church named Kyle McCarty, when he was only fifteen.

Kyle's Poem

God doesn't love me
You can't force me to believe
God is good
This is the One Truth in life
This world is a product of chance
How can I believe that
God will use my life
I know with certainty that
God has left me
Never again will I say that
Christ is risen from the dead
I know now more than ever in my life that
Man can save himself
We must realize that it is ignorant to think
God answers prayers

Christians declare that
Without God this world would fall into darkness
This world can and will meet my needs
It is a lie to say that
God has always been there for me
I now realize that
No matter what I do
The Truth is
He doesn't love me
How can I presume that
God is good

Okay, now before you think I've lost my mind or abandoned everything I've told you up to this point, I'm going to ask that you read this poem one more time. Only this time, as you read it, I'd like to ask you to make one slight change: read it backward.

Begin at the last line and read backward to the first line.

Take your time. I'll wait here.

Wow, now that makes quite a difference, doesn't it?

So much of what we go through works just like this poem. All we can see is what's right in front of us. We can't tell why God would allow such suffering and injustice in our lives or in the world around us.

But with time, with patience, with perspective, we begin to see things differently. We realize, usually in hindsight, that God has brought something amazing and totally unexpected out of the ashes of our loss, grief, and heartache.

Not least of which is a stronger faith, borne out of a deeper love for him.

Habakkuk knew that our perspective changes, even while God's remains the same.

"Though the fig tree does not bud and there are no grapes on the vines, though the olive crop fails and the fields produce no food, though there are no sheep in the pen and no cattle in the stalls, yet I will rejoice in the LORD, I will be joyful in God my Savior" (Hab. 3:17–18).

Yet I will rejoice in the Lord.

No matter what.

Conclusion

When You Question
and Believe

*Endurance is not just the ability to bear a
hard thing, but to turn it into glory.*
—William Barclay, Scottish minister

It wasn't supposed to happen.

Amy's brother, David, had gone into the hospital on Christmas Eve for some respiratory problems. He had a bad cold, and his doctor wanted to make sure it didn't develop into pneumonia or anything more severe. They knew, as we all did, that her brother, who was thirty-four, was susceptible to all kinds of infections because of his compromised immune system.

After a week, he was still in the hospital and not getting better. A few days later he took a turn for the worse. Amy and I and our entire family had been praying, of course, the whole time. But now we all called in every person we knew to help pray. I reached out to other pastor friends and their churches around the world, asking everyone to pray for our loved one.

David's story was an amazing one, and I just knew that God was going to continue to use him in miraculous ways. Having come out of a dark life filled with pain and rebellion, David had turned back to Christ and had become not just a strong believer but a great man of God, a husband, a dad, and a worship leader. David passionately loved God, and he wanted others to know what he had been through so they would be encouraged that God could (and would) help them through their own trials.

Surely, God would heal such a powerful ambassador, wouldn't he?

We continued praying as another week came and went. At one point, I estimated that tens of thousands of people around the globe were praying for David's recovery. God was going to heal my brother-in-law. I just knew it.

Only he didn't.

David died a few days later.

We were all devastated.

God had not come through in the way that any of us wanted.

As hard as it was, I helped preach at David's funeral. I cannot tell you how painful it was to see the tears in my wife's eyes, and in the eyes of everyone else in our family. We still didn't understand—and we realized we might never comprehend—why God had not answered our prayers. But even through all our grief, we were grateful that God had changed David's life and welcomed him home. With that odd mixture of sadness and gratitude, I decided to preach the gospel.

That's exactly what David would have wanted. And that's exactly what our God would have wanted.

I knew there would be lots of extended family present— including some who rarely came to church—which was all the more reason why I wanted to share the truth about God's grace and the sacrifice of Jesus on the cross. As tragic and irrational as David's death seemed, I wanted to do everything in my power to let his loss become a catalyst to get others thinking about where they stood with God.

And God moved in a powerful way. Dozens of people made decisions to trust Jesus with their hearts and lives that day. It wasn't just their emotions from the grief of losing David. The Holy Spirit was tangibly at work in that service. No one could miss it. Not that it made our sadness over losing David any easier, but there was a special comfort in knowing that God was using his life—and death—to draw people to Christ and to impact everyone there in a way too deep to describe.

I share this story with you because it's one of the simplest and most powerful experiences I've had of feeling that Habakkuk kind of faith that we've been talking about, the kind that both embraces and wrestles, the kind that questions God and yet trusts him. As much as I miss having David here with us, I can't deny that God has indeed continued to use his passing as an opportunity to draw many people closer to him, people who otherwise would not have heard and listened to the good news of the gospel.

Years later Amy mentioned that she was missing her brother. We talked about it for a while, and when I felt the moment was right, I asked her something I'd been wondering about for quite some time. "I think we both agree that God used David's life and death to impact so many people," I began. She nodded yes. "But, Amy, if we could have him back with us here on earth, only we'd have to give up all the good that God did, would you make that trade?"

Without hesitation, Amy replied firmly, "Absolutely not. I will see David again in heaven one day, and tons more people because of what God did through him. God's plan was and always is good."

And then we both cried and thanked God that his ways are higher than ours.

I DON'T KNOW WHAT YOU'RE GOING THROUGH OR WHAT YOU'VE already survived. And none of us knows what we'll face tomorrow. But I do know this: our God is a good God who loves us enough to sacrifice his precious Son, the greatest gift he could give us, just so we can know him, just so we can glorify him on earth, just so we can spend eternity with him in heaven.

He loves us that much. We're able to love him—or anyone else—only because he first loved us (1 John 4:19).

When hard things happen, and the best you can manage is to want to believe, that's enough. Don't stop wanting to believe.

Allow that spark of hope to grow by trusting that God is right there beside you. Like the father of the boy who was possessed, pray and ask God to help you overcome your unbelief. Like Habakkuk, ask your questions and then be prepared to listen to God's response.

You may have noticed that the book of Habakkuk has three short chapters. In the first, Habakkuk is doubting. In the second, he's waiting. In the third, he's embracing the goodness of God.

My prayer is that you would grow to have that Habakkuk kind of faith we see in chapter 3. But here's the deal: you can't have a chapter 3 type of faith until you've had a chapter 1 type of question and a chapter 2 kind of waiting. Because God does more spiritually in the valley than he does on the mountaintop.

Those who are closest to God have gotten there only because they keep climbing the path of faith out of the valleys in their lives. Instead of trying to run back, retracing their steps to some former peak, they've leaned into the hardships and wrestled with God, questioning him and yet trusting that he is good, that he will use everything to achieve his purposes, and that he will bring them back out—stronger, better, and closer to him than ever before. They know it's this process that ulti- mately proves God's faithfulness, character, goodness, and love.

I don't have all the answers to your questions. But after loving God and serving Christ for more than twenty-nine years now, here's what I *can* say: I've walked with Jesus for enough yesterdays to trust him with all my tomorrows. As simple as that may sound to you, I sincerely hope and pray that you can experience that same security. If not now, then one day soon.

Do you want to grow closer to God? Do you want that intimacy with him more than you want a comfortable, easygoing, problem-free life?

Do you want to know that he is with you and cares about you, no matter what you are going through?

Then doubt all you want, but never stop believing. Or at least wanting to believe.

You can have hope in the dark. Because as you grow to know God, he will reveal even more of his love, his faithfulness, his grace. And over time you will realize, believe, and embrace that even when life is difficult, God is still good.

Questions for Reflection

INTRODUCTION

Read Mark 9:14–29.

In the introduction, we looked briefly at the story of the father and struggling son. The dad wanted to believe that Jesus could help his son, but because nothing had happened, the dad struggled to have faith that Jesus could do anything about his problem.

Question 1: Where in your life are you struggling to believe that God can do something?

Question 2: What do you think could build your faith to believe that God is with you and that he can help?

PART 1: HIDE AND SEEK

1.1: Where Are You, God?

Read Psalm 6:2–3, 6–7 and Matthew 27:45–46.

The authors of Job, Lamentations, Ecclesiastes, and Jeremiah all expressed doubts. In some Christian circles, we are almost discouraged from expressing any real and sincere doubts. The implied message is that if you ever doubt, you don't have real faith.

> Question 1: When have you doubted God's involvement or goodness?
>
> Question 2: Have your doubts ever eventually helped strengthen your faith? Explain.

1.2: Why Don't You Care?
Read Habakkuk 1:2–4.

> How long, LORD, must I call for help,
>> but you do not listen?
> Or cry out to you, "Violence!"
>> but you do not save?
> Why do you make me look at injustice?
>> Why do you tolerate wrongdoing?
> Destruction and violence are before me;
>> there is strife, and conflict abounds.
> Therefore the law is paralyzed,
>> and justice never prevails.
> The wicked hem in the righteous,
>> so that justice is perverted.
>
> —Habakkuk 1:2–4

It's easy to trust God when things are going our way. But when something happens that we consider unfair, doubt often creeps in. Habakkuk wrestled with questions of injustice. He essentially asked God, "Why do we cry out but you don't do anything? Why do you tolerate their wrongdoing? Why do you let criminals go unpunished while the innocent suffer?" If you have ever wrestled with apparent injustices, you are not alone.

Question 1: What are some of the injustices you see around you today (in your personal life, in your community, nationally, and globally)?

Question 2: How do these apparent injustices impact your faith in God? Be honest.

1.3: Why Aren't You Doing Something?
Read Psalm 56:8.

David cried, "Record my misery; list my tears on your scroll—are they not in your record?" Notice how in Psalm 56 and in so many other psalms, David cried out to God honestly, in anguish and deep desperation. So often, Christians are afraid to be open and honest with God (as if he doesn't already know our thoughts). But David and even Jesus didn't hold back when they were hurting. God is certainly big enough to handle our cries and questions. What if he prefers that, instead of pretending that everything is okay when it's really not, we run to him with honest, open, hurting hearts?

Question 1: When was the last time you honestly questioned God or expressed your anger toward him? How did you feel afterward?

Question 2: What in your life right now do you need to take to God? Do you have any honest doubts? Deep frustrations? Disappointments? What's holding you back from complete honesty with God?

1.4: It Seems Unfair
Read Psalm 10:1–18.

Habakkuk wasn't afraid to ask the really difficult questions. As we noted earlier, the Hebrew word used to describe Habakkuk's message is *massa*, which means "an ominous utterance, a doom, a burden." To strengthen our faith, God doesn't just use ordinary and normal events; occasionally he uses an ominous utterance, a doom, a burden. In the book, I asked, "What if drawing closer to God, developing genuine intimacy with him, requires you to bear something that feels unbearable? To hear him through an ominous utterance, to trust him in the moment of doom, to embrace his strength when you're weak with a burden? What if it takes real pain to experience deep and abiding hope?"

Question 1: Describe a time when God used something painful to get your attention and ultimately draw you closer to him.
Question 2: What struggle are you facing now? (This could involve either you or someone you love.) What is God doing in you through this struggle? What is he teaching you?

1.5: Crisis of Belief
Read 2 Corinthians 12:6–10.

As noted earlier, Henry Blackaby describes what he calls a "crisis of belief," a season of struggling and doubting God and his goodness in our lives. These moments of struggle are often prompted by some sort of disappointment, setback, or challenge. Many well-meaning Christians say that God won't give you more than you can handle. But this simply isn't true. (The verse they are quoting is 1 Corinthians 10:13, which actually says that God won't let you be *tempted* beyond what you can handle.) God will occasionally allow you to have more than you can handle, to teach you to depend on him. If you have questions, God is big enough to handle them. Your questions may even lead you to depend on him in ways you haven't before

Question 1: What question do you have for God about your current situation?

Question 2: Chances are good that your question for God starts with "Why." Maybe it is, "Why did you allow . . . ?" or "Why didn't you . . . ?" Can you ask a different question, but this time start with "What"? You might ask, "What are you showing me?" or "What is your purpose in allowing . . . ?"

PART 2: LOST AND FOUND

2.1: Listen

Read Psalm 46:10 and John 10:1–5.

When things aren't going our way, most of us talk to God about what bothers us. But perhaps an even more valuable discipline is to talk to God and then listen. Jesus even said in John 10 that we would know his voice.

> Question 1: Describe a time when you believe that you heard from God. Maybe he directed you with his Word, prompted you by his Spirit, blessed you with a song, or comforted you through a friend.
>
> Question 2: When was the last time you stopped everything and just sat completely still, listening for God's voice? What happened when you did?

2.2: Write

Read Habakkuk 2:2.

God told Habakkuk, "Write down the revelation and make it plain on tablets so that a herald may run with it" (Hab. 2:2).

When I was a new Christian, a friend gave me a new Bible with my name engraved on it. Immediately he challenged me to underline my favorite verse and to write the date out to the side of the verse on that page. I recall not wanting to write in the Bible but to instead keep it new and clean. He explained that taking notes in the Bible about what I was learning and about verses I'd want to revisit later would become one of the greatest tools for my spiritual growth. And he was right! Now, years later, I have too many notes to count, written all over pages in various paper Bibles and linked to passages in my YouVersion Bible app.

> Question 1: What is something that God has shown you recently that you don't want to forget? Would you

commit to writing it down? If you're hesitating, ask yourself, "Why wouldn't I?"

Question 2: Do you have a place or a method for recording the lessons, truths, and revelations that you receive from God? If so, describe it. If not, what could you do to keep and treasure those powerful gifts? (Hints: a written journal, an online service, an app on your phone.)

2.3: Wait

Read Psalm 27:13–14, Lamentations 3:25, and Isaiah 40:31.

I don't know anyone who enjoys waiting. If a program is slow to download or a line at the store is too long, I'm quick to move on. But with God, many of the biggest blessings are on the other side of the wait. I read a quote that said, "Joseph waited fifteen years, Abraham waited twenty-five years, Moses waited forty years, and Jesus waited thirty years. If you're waiting, you're in very good company."

Question 1: What is something that you wish God would do *now*, but as far as you can tell, he wants you to wait?

Question 2: A waiter or waitress is one who serves. Some people think that waiting on God means we aren't doing anything. But waiting on God is the perfect time to serve him. What do you think God wants you to do while you're waiting?

2.4: By Faith

Read Hebrews 11 (often called the Faith Hall of Fame).

We know that without faith, it's impossible to please God (Heb. 11:6). And Paul taught that we should walk by faith and not by sight (2 Cor. 5:7).

Question 1: What area or situation in your life right now is demanding the most faith?

Question 2: How much faith do you have for God to be involved in this situation? (Even if it's not much, remember: God can do a lot with a little. See Matthew 17:20.)

2.5: "Faith Tested"

Read 1 Peter 1:3–9.

Most people don't like tests. But passing a test is often what builds our faith and helps us move forward spiritually.

Question 1: Describe a time when your faith was tested and eventually strengthened. Did you have seasons of doubt during that trial? What kept you going? How did God use the trial to grow your faith?

Question 2: Are you currently going through something that might be a test? What do you think God is showing you?

PART 3: HOPE AND GLORY

3.1: Remember

God tells us to remember what we were before we met Christ (Eph. 2:11–13), to remember his covenant (1 Chron. 16:15;

Gen. 9:14–16; Ps. 111:5), and to remember the death and resurrection of Christ (1 Cor. 11:24–26).

Read Lamentations 3:21–24.

> Yet I still dare to hope
> > when I *remember* this:
> The faithful love of the LORD never ends!
> > His mercies never cease.
> Great is his faithfulness;
> > his mercies begin afresh each morning.
> I say to myself, "The LORD is my inheritance;
> > therefore, I will hope in him!"
> > > —Lamentations 3:21–24 NLT, emphasis mine

It's obvious that it's important to God that we do not forget to remember.

Question 1: Describe who you were and what you were like before you met the grace of Christ. Describe how your life changed because of who Christ is and because of what he did for you on the cross.

Question 2: What are your three favorite God moments (times when you knew that God was with you or working on your behalf or revealing himself to you in a special way)?

3.2: Accept

Habakkuk heard difficult news from God. Although he might have wanted to pretend otherwise, it was in his best interest to accept the truth and face the music. Not everything goes our way. Noah didn't hope for a flood. Jonah didn't dream about being swallowed by a fish. David didn't dream of one day facing a giant. Someone said, "What you deny or ignore, you delay. But what you accept and face, you conquer." You don't have to understand the why to trust and accept God's heart and intentions.

> Question 1: I read a quote recently that said, "Grace is accepting what is instead of resenting what isn't." What does this mean to you?
> Question 2: Describe a reality, either current or in your past, that you may have denied but that God wants you to accept.

3.3: Trust
Read Habakkuk 3:16–18.

> I heard and my heart pounded,
>> my lips quivered at the sound;
> decay crept into my bones,
>> and my legs trembled.
> Yet I will wait patiently for the day of calamity
>> to come on the nation invading us.
> Though the fig tree does not bud
>> and there are no grapes on the vines,
> though the olive crop fails
>> and the fields produce no food,

though there are no sheep in the pen
and no cattle in the stalls,
yet I will rejoice in the LORD,
I will be joyful in God my Savior.

—Habakkuk 3:16–18

I love the depth of Habakkuk's faith and trust. He essentially says, "Even though I don't like it, even though I don't understand it, even though I know he could and he should but he's not, yet will I trust in the Lord my God."

Question 1: How are you growing in your faith to trust in God's character and not in your circumstances? Explain.

Question 2: Share about a time when you were disappointed in your circumstances, but you had complete faith and trust in God's goodness.

3.4: Hope

After facing all of the challenges that he knew were coming, Habakkuk turned his heart fully to God with this statement of faith: "The Sovereign LORD is my strength; he makes my feet like the feet of a deer, he enables me to tread on the heights" (Hab. 3:19).

Question 1: Describe what it is that gives you hope for the future. Is it promises from God's Word? God's faithfulness in your past? His grace in the present? Or something else? If you don't have hope for the future, be honest and talk about it with someone.

Question 2: Habakkuk said that the Lord makes his feet like that of a deer and enables him to tread on new heights. How has God helped you grow in the past? What do you sense God doing to prepare you for the future?

3.5: Believe

The Proverbs tell us, "Where there is no vision, the people perish" (29:18 KJV). There's something about the power of hope that fuels us and enables us to persevere. Even Jesus continued past his own hesitation in the garden of Gethsemane, faithful to God all the way to his death on the cross. What kept him going? Hebrews says it was "the joy set before him" (Heb. 12:2). It's amazing what we can endure when we have a reason.

Question 1: If you've ever felt like giving up, going away, or checking out, what keeps you going?

Question 2: Paul said in Romans 5:3–4, "We also glory in our sufferings, because we know that suffering produces perseverance; perseverance, character; and character, hope." Explain how you have seen God reveal this truth in your life.

Conclusion

In Romans 8:28, Paul tells us that "God works for the good of those who love him, who have been called according to his purpose." Sometimes in the middle of our trials, it's difficult to see what's good. But after time passes, we often can look back and see how God's lovingkindness paved a way through our pain to something good.

Question 1: As you reflect on your life, how can you now see that God was faithfully working for your good during a season of hardship or struggle?

Question 2: Based on how you've seen God bring good out of the past, what do you think he might be doing in your present to help you become more like Christ?

Acknowledgments

I'd like to express my deepest gratitude to all my friends who helped make this book possible.

Amy Groeschel, serving Jesus with you is by far my favorite part of life.

Catie (and Andrew), Mandy (and James), Anna, Sam, Stephen, and Joy, you serve our Savior. You bring me joy. You make me proud.

Dudley Delffs, how many books have we done together now? I'm thankful for each one because I've grown to love you more with every project.

David Morris, Lyn Cryderman, Brandon Henderson, Tom Dean, John Raymond, Brian Phipps, and the whole team at Zondervan, it's truly an honor to publish with you. You honor Jesus with the work you do, and it shows.

Tom Winters, you are a great friend and a brilliant agent.

Brannon Golden, your family inspires me. And your editing is spooky good.

Tanner Keim, thank you for covering so many details and serving our church with passion. You are a crazy good assistant. (I told you that you would be.)

And Adrianne Manning, you can't ever leave my office, or I will have to go with you. Your family is my family. This book is for you.

 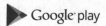

Hundreds of millions of people are using the *YouVersion Bible App* to make God's Word a part of their daily lives.

Download the free app and access your bookmarks, notes, and reading plans from anywhere. Enjoy hundreds of versions, including audio, all on your mobile device.